BY THE SAME
AUTHOR

SCENES
FROM
RUSSIAN
LIFE

VLADIMIR SOLOUKHIN

LAUGHTER OVER THE LEFT SHOULDER

TRANSLATED FROM THE RUSSIAN BY DAVID MARTIN

U.S. DISTRIBUTOR
DUFOUR EDITIONS
CHESTER SPRINGS,
PA 19425-0449
(215) 458-5005

PETER OWEN

London and Chester Springs PA

NEITHER IN ENVIRONMENT NOR IN HEREDITY CAN I FIND
THE EXACT INSTRUMENT THAT FASHIONED ME,
THE ANONYMOUS ROLLER THAT PRESSED UPON MY LIFE
A CERTAIN INTRICATE WATERMARK
WHOSE UNIQUE DESIGN BECOMES VISIBLE
WHEN THE LAMP OF ART IS MADE TO SHINE
THROUGH LIFE'S FOOLSCAP.

VLADIMIR NABOKOV

PETER OWEN PUBLISHERS
73 Kenway Road   London SW5 0RE
Peter Owen books are distributed in the USA by
Dufour Editions Inc. Chester Springs PA

Originally published as *Smekh za levym plechom*
First published in Great Britain 1990
© Possev-Verlag, V. Gorachek KG, 1988
Frankfurt am Main
English translation © David Martin 1990

British Library Cataloguing in Publication Data
Soloukhin, Vladimir, *1924–*
Laughter over the left shoulder.
1. Prose in Russian. Soloukhin, Vladimir, 1924–
I. Title
891.784408

ISBN 0–7206–0798–1

Printed in Great Britain by Billings of Worcester

1

I APPEARED OUT OF NOTHINGNESS TOWARDS THE END OF A warm June night. Without a doubt, the first earthly sounds I heard were the harsh cries of rooks. They always cry at that time.

Thirty paces from our two-storey house with its iron roof are the church railings: a brick base and pillars, the railings themselves of wrought iron, small corner towers with crosses on them. Limes grow all around them. The trees were planted by my grandfather, Aleksey Dmitrievich. Two small crosses poke out from the mass of limes, one on the church, the other on the bell-tower. If the limes nearest to our house do not completely overhang it – that is, so that their tops tower above the roof – then they almost do; and in the limes are colonies of rooks' nests. The rooks simply must have been crying that night.

(Is that the reason why I still fall asleep in my house regardless of the racket made by the rooks, whereas friends who come to stay, unable to sleep, suffer, curse the rooks and are even surprised that I have put up with them all this time and have not sent their nests crashing to the ground or in some way exterminated these raucous birds? My nerves are no less battered and frayed than those of my friends who come to stay. I cannot get to sleep myself if a tap drips above the sink or the wind rattles an open window; but the deafening, frantic cry of the rooks I somehow do not hear at all. I sleep soundly beneath the roof of that very same house in which I emerged from nothingness once on a warm June night.)

My soul, wavering, having joined neither the forces of darkness nor those of the light, unable to choose or perceive which side to take, flew through creation, condemned to life on earth, hurled down by a higher will into the gaping black void. Following the rules, it has already forgotten everything that went beforehand and knows nothing of what is to come. It is deaf, blind and dumb. It is nothing. It has been disconnected from the central will and rushes on simply with the power of inertia imparted to it when it was first cast forth. One thing is not clear: will it fall wide of the village, the house and the tiny lump of matter which is to be its new abode and which has been prepared for its use during the whole of the test period? If it misses, it will go slap into a bog, the calm, deep water of the river or a well, and then they will say that the child was stillborn.

But the timing has been adjusted to a split second, exact directions have been given and on it flies.

How will they get on together, the eternal soul and its new, if only temporary dwelling? Which one will torture the other and which give the other delight? 'Little by little the eternal soul came to value its temporary body.' That line of poetry did not exist then.

Now there is a kind of blueness ahead and all around. A slow but steep descent begins. The global curvature of the earth approaches. There are oceans, continents and peoples. The target it is meant to hit is really microscopic. The entire population of a country would be fine, as would be a town, but this. . . . And how will it fit into a dwelling of such meagre proportions if it itself is virtually infinite?

But at the moment it is disconnected from the central will and is therefore limited, localized. During flight, moreover, it is reduced to nil. It has been artificially deprived of any memory of the past and knowledge of the future. There is total darkness and total silence. Nothingness.

The earth, where it will have to undergo the trials which await it, rushes towards it. It flattens out. Then its edges bend again, only upwards this time. It begins to resemble a shallow bowl filled to the brim with moonlight.

The soul must not miss its target. Two crosses poke through the mass of trees and make a wonderful landmark. A little to the right is the roof of the house, glittering with dew and moonlight. The yellowish light of a paraffin lamp shines through an open window on the upstairs floor. People are fussing about, water is being heated. On a wide bed with boards of walnut veneer at the head and foot a woman is tossing and turning. The church cross, the limes, the iron roof and the window have been left behind. . . . The headlong flight completes its trajectory and is over, like a star falling in the summer sky or the track of a tracer bullet that has reached its mark. There is one last moment of darkness, silence and nothingness. . . . Smack! The silence bursts, exploding with the deafening cry of rooks in the old limes.

Other earthly sounds immediately appeared, too. Somebody said: 'Well then, it's over. It's a boy. Congratulations.'

And Stepanida Ivanovna raised her eyes upwards, even though she was lying on her back as it was, and whispered feebly: 'God be praised! God be praised!'

After this a high-pitched, lusty cry was heard. The cry of the soul itself. Perhaps it cried when it first felt the unaccustomed tightness of its new dwelling; perhaps it immediately realized the total cruelty of the sentence and the torment of the trial that awaited. Perhaps, on the other hand, it cried for joy at not missing its mark and because the absolute darkness and silence had ended and the state of total nothingness was over. Now there were the strident cries of the rooks, the whisper throughout the house that it's a boy, the diffuse light of the paraffin lamp. The latter, incidentally, was no longer necessary, as it was already daytime. Now there was being.

2

THE PREVIOUS DAY HAD BEEN BRIGHT AND FESTIVE. IT WAS
the Day of the Holy Trinity.[1] The country folk had gone
to church – the men in caps with shiny peaks, the women
in white spotted or, perhaps, floral headscarves. They
carried flowers. There were flowers on the floor of the
church. The icons were decorated with flowers and the
houses in the village with young birch twigs.

On that particular day there had been a church festival in
the neighbouring market town of Cherkutino (a large town
compared with ours), where the church was dedicated to the
Holy Trinity. Masses of people had been out and about,
both in the village itself and in Kleshchikovaya grove, a
birch wood one kilometre from Cherkutino. My sisters,
grown girls, had been enjoying themselves during the day
in Kleshchikovaya grove as well as in Cherkutino. There
was Klavdia, twenty-one years old and a former pupil of the
Model Grammar School for Girls in the provincial capital of
Vladimir; Tonya, twenty; Valentina, seventeen (in a few days
time she was to become my godmother); and Katyusha, who
was sixteen. I dare say they had been wearing bright hats,
perhaps of straw, with ribbons and equally bright summer
dresses. Towards evening on the Day of the Holy Trinity
they had seen their father, Aleksey Alekseevich, ride up in
his light tarantass, drawn by Golubchik, and stop at the
house of Dr Nikolay Vasilyevich Lebedev. The doctor's wife,

1 The author's and translator's notes appear on pp. 150–2

8

Elizaveta Pavlovna, who was also the midwife, had got into the tarantass to be borne off with a gentle springing motion in the direction of Alepino.

We used to think that this had all happened on the night of 13th/14th June, and consequently I always believed that my date of birth was 14th June. That is what it says on all those forms I have had to fill in and in various biographical notes concerning me, including those in the *Great Soviet Encyclopaedia* and in a reference book published in many volumes somewhere in England and known by the title of *Who's Who*.

One day, however, Lyuda Grebenshchikova, a fine lyric poet whom I helped with the publication of her first book, telephoned me.

'Vladimir Alekseevich, I have here an almanac covering the whole period from the sixteenth to the twenty-second centuries. You were born on the 14th June 1924. That was a Saturday. Listen to what the Japanese horoscope says about the personal qualities of people born on a Saturday . . .'

'My dear Lyudmila Anatolyevna, thank you for your call and your interest, but the thing is I couldn't have been born on a Saturday. Not at all!'

'Don't you believe it! The 14th June 1924 was a Saturday.'

'I wasn't born on 14th June, then.'

'Why?'

'Because I was born on the Day of the Holy Spirit. That's a feast-day. It's always on the day after the Day of the Holy Trinity. That's always a Sunday. The date changes with Easter, but it's always a Sunday. The Day of the Holy Spirit is always a Monday. Do you see?'

'But what makes you so sure about the Day of the Holy Spirit?'

'I just am. . . . In our family they could forget or make a mistake with a date but not with a feast-day. During the day my sisters had been out and about in Cherkutino, you see. That was the Day of the Holy Trinity. They saw

9

Aleksey Alekseevich ride up in his carriage for Elizaveta Pavlovna . . .'

'Who is this Elizaveta Pavlovna?'

'The midwife. Don't you see? I was born during the night, actually, in the small hours of Monday morning rather than on Sunday night. It was the Day of the Holy Spirit.'

'On the 16th, then? So, what are you going to do about it?'

'What, indeed.' Then I had a thought. 'You know what? I'll turn my birthday into a movable feast . . .'

'Meaning?'

'You know. . . . The Day of the Holy Trinity is movable, as is the Day of the Holy Spirit. This year, for example . . . let me think. . . . Easter was the 30th April . . . add seven weeks. . . . The Day of the Holy Trinity will be the 18th June and the Day of the Holy Spirit the 19th. This year, then, I'll celebrate my birthday on the 19th June. Next year it will be, let's say, the 11th June. . . . Wonderful! But every year it will be on the Day of the Holy Spirit. Do you understand?'

Lyudmila Anatolyevna, fine lyric poet that she was, understood everything.

3

AND SO – SMACK! THE SHELL OF NON-BEING BREAKS AND the rooks cry.

The earth on which I found myself had plenty of reason to be called at one and the same time both heaven and hell. That is understandable when you remember the chief reason why I was cast down there: if in the end I had to choose between two extremes, then those extremes had to be present and I needed the opportunity to have a good look at them.

At that moment I could not see the pure, white, sweet-scented damask violets flowering beneath the cool forest canopy in the quiet of the June night, nor the moths which visited them on the wing, shining green as they flashed into pools of moonlight or fading in patches of darkness. Nor could I even see the luxuriant jasmin beneath the windows with its seasonal covering of fragrant white flowers. Nor, on that same June night, could I see or hear any better those innocent people who were dying in prisons and camps, suffering before death or being shot in the back of the head in OGPU basements, the latter form of death being considered humane in comparison with a bullet through the forehead or heart.

It was June 1924. The damask violets were certainly in flower, the moths were certainly flying in the quiet of the moonlit forest and people were certainly suffering and being murdered that night.

As a new-born infant I could neither see nor know anything; but had I been able, upon first finding myself

11

on earth, to take an immediate look around me, like an astronaut who has landed on another planet, I should have had to conclude right from the start that I was in heaven. If, on the other hand, I could at the very same time have inwardly perceived everything that was happening on the planet, I should have been aghast and promptly realized that I had been thrown into hell.

If they summoned together the most gifted artists and told them that there existed in the universe a bare rock which had to be variously adorned, so that the effect would be sublime and possess a beauty capable of arousing noble and kind feelings, a beauty which would make people better and purer and never become tedious, and the artists rolled up their sleeves and set to work, well, could they really think up anything finer than the sky which surrounds this´ earth, with its moon and sun, stars and clouds, its rainbows and all the many hues of its sunsets and sunrises? Could they really think of anything finer than the earth's seas, mountains, rivers, lakes, waterfalls, trees or flowers?

If they summoned together the most skilful torturers and said, look, we have to equip a kind of laboratory, an establishment for inflicting agony and torture on people, well, could they really think up anything as sophisticated and varied as the collection of tortures that hounds us all our lives?

The fear of losing your children or any of your near ones is torture; actually losing your children and near ones and burying them in the earth is torture. It is torture when parents, unable to help or do anything, watch their children starve; illnesses and fear torture you, as does the constant awareness of mortality and the impossibility of achieving your desires. You can be tortured by jealousy, wounded pride, the realization of other people's superiority, helpless fury, hunger, thirst and insatiability. It is torture to be subjected to coercion, to be humiliated, insulted, to experience unrequited love and the ingratitude of your children or of people as a whole. Permanent involuntary work is torture, as are both the threat and reality of poverty. You can be tortured by unrelieved boredom, anguish, anxiety, cold, heat, the pointlessness of existence, suicide, infanticide, parricide, fratricide. . . .

There is no denying that both extremes were right there, together in time and space, and an entire lifetime is exactly what it takes to comprehend them both; that is, the great beauty of the earth along with the great evil which dominates it. And so a whole life has been given me to comprehend both the one and the other.

Luckily, as I was about to set off on my many years' journey through life's vale, I was given a compass at which, unfortunately, I glanced less and less often as the years went by. There were even years when I did not look at it at all, just as if it did not exist.

I clearly remember the lesson concerning the two extremes of earthly existence that my mother gave me at the very start of it all. In my opinion neither the professors who taught me later nor the writers whose books I have managed to read have supplied me with a view of things as lucid and impressive as Stepanida Ivanovna's. 'Wherever you go and whatever you do,' she would say, 'there is always an angel standing at your right shoulder. But Satan' – she called him 'the Cunning One' – 'is standing at your left shoulder. They see everything you do and even know what you are thinking. And so, when you do anything good or kind – let's say you stand up for someone who is being treated badly, give to those in need, help your mother and father, feed a hungry cat or cross yourself before going to sleep at night – then the angel at your right shoulder smiles with joy, but the Cunning One winces and wriggles as if he were being fried. But if you do something wrong – say, ill-treat some little girl, an old lady or anyone weaker than you are, or you upset your mother and father, turn lazy or torture a kitten – then the angel at your right shoulder will weep bitter tears and the Cunning One will gloat and giggle.'

'Why will he giggle?'

'Because it is all his doing. You did something bad when

he whispered in your ear and you were silly enough to do as he said. And so you are in his power and he is overjoyed. There he is, sniggering away and rubbing his hands.'

'So why doesn't the angel whisper in my ear to make me do good things?'

'The angel makes suggestions, too, only we listen to him less.'

'Why?'

'Because the other of the pair – his enemy – is the Cunning One. . . . And so they will be pulling you in different directions all your life. One of them will try to destroy you, the other will try to save you.'

That night as I lay awake I promised to myself that my angel would always be laughing and full of joy, whilst the Cunning One at my left shoulder would be left writhing about and gnashing his teeth. Of my subtler psychological reactions to all this, the one to single out here was: how could I possibly let my angel down or, so to speak, fail to justify his trust in me?

4

THE HOUSE, ORCHARD, VILLAGE AND EVERYTHING ELSE THAT could be seen from the roof as far as the horizon – that was the area of planet which, with its variety of features (a winding river, small pine and fir woods on the hills, ravines, meadows and fields), had been allotted to me for my earthly existence.

Of these three constituents – the house, orchard and surrounding area – I shall take my recollections of the orchard first.

Strictly speaking, it would of course be true to say that the brighter the sun shone at midday, the brighter it was in our yard. The gold of the summer outside penetrated through all the little holes in the awning and through various cracks, to stretch out in straw-yellow lines across the entire yard or lie in playful oval patches of light. Yet, despite this, the relative effect was such as to make the yard seem darker and cooler the brighter and hotter it was outside. This on occasion meant that, when the small gate at the bottom of the yard, leading to the orchard, was opened, there was such a blinding radiance that it would have been impossible to look at it were it not for the lush green glow of grass and leaves which was to be seen further on and which was soft and cool to the eyes.

When you go through the back gate of any peasant yard, you enter of course a world of vegetable patches full of cucumbers, carrots and onions; but at our place you fell into the embrace, as it were, of a huge jasmin. It was tall and mighty, a miracle of sweet-scented white blossoms. It was as if a swan had landed by mistake among domestic fowl like chickens and geese. True, he was not alone in landing there, because next to him were small beds in which white lilies and narcissi bloomed.

(Now, with the disorderly intermingling of various social spheres and strata or, rather, now that everything has become a jumbled mishmash, the presence of flowers like these in a peasant's kitchen garden could not possibly be thought of as a miracle or even as a rare exception, but at that time that is exactly what it was – an exception and a miracle, as if an ermine cape had appeared from nowhere and was hanging on the coat-rack alongside a sheepskin coat, a light cloth coat and a peaked cap.)

A narrow, well-trodden path led from the gate, past the jasmin, lilies and narcissi (doubtless, there were other flowers growing there, too – asters, chrysanthemums, dahlias, but they have slipped my memory), and on into the depths of the orchard. I recall this path not primarily for the way it looked, but for its effect on the soles of my bare feet. The point is that the part of our yard used by vehicles was paved with large stones from the river. These were cold no matter how hot the weather. Never mind your bare feet, you had to walk over these rounded, damp and ice-cold stones before you reached the orchard. For me as a child, the simple transition from these stones to the warm, friendly earth of the path to the orchard was a real event.

Even now, with the skin of my feet separated from the ground by very nearly an inch of top quality rubber or, if it comes to it, crêpe, I vividly recall the permanent cold of those stones – it even penetrated as far as my ankles – followed by that sudden, joyful warmth which went straight to the heart. The grass that brushed my knees was also cool, but it was a different sort of coolness and unlike the cold of the stones.

The path went away into the depths of the orchard . . . . But you have to imagine the scale of things there. In Grandfather's orchard there were twenty-six apple trees.

16

True, apart from them, there was one plum tree, a patch of raspberries (coming up to ten paces square), there were blackcurrant bushes growing by the palings around the vegetable plot (I should think there would be up to fifteen of them), and some cherries. One spot consisted of an impenetrable jungle of prickly trees and blackthorn bushes.

And Adam also ate of the apple. His temptress in paradise might have offered him a heavy bunch of grapes (reminiscent, by the way, of a woman's breast and therefore as a symbol closer to love than an apple), or any other fruit, even a nut, which would have also symbolized female nature – not long ago a certain person from Moscow who takes an interest in the subject was saying that you have to discover what a woman is really like before anything else and that there are apparently some tough nuts to crack.

No, the fruit was there not merely to be discovered, but tasted properly; and pecking away a berry at a time would have been useless where you needed to sink your teeth in. The apple is the fruit of fruits and the first woman, offering all the sweetness of the world to the first man, could hold out in her open palms nothing else, not a pear, or a quince, or a persimmon, or any of your exotic mangoes and avocados.

In Grandfather's paradise of an orchard grew twenty-six thoroughbred Russian apple trees, their pedigrees unaffected by Michurin's later incestuous concoctions. There were Antonovkas, Grushovkas, Borovinkas, Anisovkas, fresh whites and cinnamon apples, as well as one other apple tree which we called the lime apple because the translucence, aroma and sweetness of its fruit resembled lime honey. It was as if someone had poured the honey into, let us say, a delicate, top-quality wineglass and placed pips at its centre.

The orchard was not huge, but it was full of hidden nooks. Apart from that, one can be sure that a child saw it differently from adults. The adults knew that a cinnamon apple stood in this spot and a Grushovka in that, and that

17

was enough. But the child lived in a world of close-ups. He knew all about the knot in the apple-tree trunk on which he put his foot when he wanted to climb up it; he knew the rough and smooth areas of trunk and the places where it bent, forked or contained a hollow. Every apple tree had its small distinctive marks and a look all of its own.

Whenever I entered our orchard in later years – indeed, when I enter it now (as in general when I find myself these days amidst the scenery anywhere in central Russia) – I have the impression that I am in a house in which nobody lives or a church in which there are no more services. I seem to be looking at the bed of a river where the flow of water has ceased or the bottom of a pond that has completely dried up. It is wine without potency, food without salt, a forest without birds, spring without flowers, a man without a soul, nature without spirituality. . . .

There were bees, too, in our orchard. The hives stood to the left of the path. Their back walls were turned towards the path and their entrance porches faced south into the cherry trees which at that spot formed a dense thicket. There were enough bees in Grandfather's twenty hives not only for our orchard, but for other orchards too, as well as for the old limes around the church, the cornflowers in the fields, the white willows that grew along the bank of the river and the willows that flowered in the forest during the early days of spring, enough even for the white and pink fields of buckwheat, for the places where the trees had been cut and the willow-herb grew, and for all the different flowers that bloomed in the meadows, on the strips between the fields and at the edge of the forest.

The edge of the forest, when you think about it, is as much of a paradise as an orchard. True, there are no fruits to eat there – no apples, no dates, no figs – but the soul, of course, does not live by bread alone. A juniper bush amidst a luxuriant carpet of flowers (as the sun gets warmer), birches gazing at themselves in a blue lake of flax, a soft pillow of cool moss, a butterfly quivering in its path across the airy expanse of a forest clearing – surely all that would lend a fitting décor to a place prepared for man's unbounded bliss!

Our orchard was impossibly small for twenty energetic and well-cared-for families of bees. The bees would leave their doorways, soar sharply aloft, avoiding the cherry trees which grew too close to them, and move off in black lines until they disappeared into the summer blue. Twenty hives, their little circular entrance holes pointing south, kept up a constant, uninterrupted, dawn-to-dusk bombardment of the surrounding area with little black buzzing missiles. There was possibly not a single square metre in the neighbourhood not visited by our – that is, Grandfather's – bees.

Now it has all gone to rack and ruin, waste and decay. Our orchard is still there, the grass grows and the trees blossom, but something is missing. It is somehow colourless, empty, cold and dead. Sometimes a little bee might chance to fly in, settle on a dandelion and make you even more aware of the contrast between this wretched orphanhood and the full-blooded, confident sense of well-being there used to be.

As items of hardware became superfluous they were either thrown out or kept in the house and made to perform some new, at times absurd, domestic function. The two-and-a-half gallon samovar, designed for tea drinking with guests on church holidays (after the Holy Liturgy), was turned into a wash-basin. The dirty, soapy water would trickle down through its little tap into (the same story) the large copper pan in which jam used to be made. Loathsome paraffin was kept in the shallow copper bowl that had formerly held mead. In the carved oak tallboy, where fresh linen should lie beneath a sprinkling of wild rose petals, ridiculous little glass bottles lay scattered among lamp burners, old batteries from hand torches, window bolts, bits of wire, a whetstone and some rags which had lost all semblance of anything. Even the pitchfork that had been used to turn the hay was no longer needed at all and was propping up the drooping branch of an apple tree.

An old tub which had been hollowed out of a single piece of limewood (more than a metre in diameter) found itself a place in the corner of the yard as a nesting-place for the hens. First the dry, bluish space inside the tub would be half filled with straw. When a depression was eventually formed at the centre of the straw by the hot, heavy weight of the sitting hen, a dummy egg would be placed in it – a white rag sewn into an oblong ball and stuffed with cotton wool. It was awkward-looking and undersized and no living being could mistake it for a real hen's egg, except for the hen herself. Perhaps, though, she was simply tolerant of it rather than indifferent or stupid. When the hen had finished sitting, a semi-transparent, warm, genuine hen's egg, faultlessly formed, totally finished and even elegant, would be left alongside this grotesque dummy.

It would not be possible to call this tub huge, had it been made from a number of sections, like all normal tubs; but it had been hollowed out of a single piece of limewood and as such might have been considered a great rarity. If one's imagination could, on the basis of that one tub, paint the whole lime, a great rustling tree would immediately arise in the mind, next to which (or beneath which) not only would the tub appear tiny, but possibly our house too would look like a toy. Green and sombre, it would spread out like a cloud and fling its branches wide across the sky. Each of these branches could itself be a full-grown tree, as it sprang from the stout and massive lower part of the trunk which later tempted the craftsman tub-maker.

It had to be sawn off and hollowed out, although all he needed for that were the tools and his hands. But what patience had been required to season the wood so that not a single crack appeared in it for decades afterwards. Perhaps even a century had passed!

The walls of the tub were not thick and its circumference

was slightly undulating. It may be that it had retained the shape of the living trunk; or perhaps after all it had warped with time.

Near the bottom was a small, round hole stopped up with a wooden bung. That means that the tub had originally been intended not for salting cucumbers or making sauerkraut but for holding some kind of liquid (which would pour out when the bung was removed). I reckon the tub would take about 250 gallons.[2]

When the old folk, deprived of their past and with no expectations for the future, were whiling away the time at the very close of their lives as best they could, this tub, then, was turned into a hens' nest. At first it was used as such, but after that it was abandoned because the hens themselves became a thing of the past. Other junk would pile up with it in the corner of the yard where it stood. The tub ended up buried beneath it all and reappeared on earth only during a thorough overhaul of the house (which will be described in these notes only after a great stretch of life has been covered). Everything rotten in the house (including the walls) had been taken and thrown to one side. Those rotten bits and pieces formed a mountain which we would not have been able to burn ourselves in ten years, so we appealed to our neighbours and they quickly took everything away to their own yards.

Later, I was passing our neighbour's house where bits of our rotting junk were piled up high like an Egyptian pyramid, when a memory suddenly burst upon me and rooted me to the spot. On the grass next to some decaying logs there stood this wonderful limewood tub, its thin walls hewn from a single piece of wood, with its undulating circumference and bluish colour (actually, it was grey, but it seemed blue). True, it no longer had a bottom but, strange though it may seem, the oaken bung had survived in its hole. It was specifically this bung that stirred my memories more than anything; before that I had had no suspicion of the existence of such memories in my mind, cluttered up as it was with later useless rubbish. I immediately saw my grandfather's hands carefully rocking the bung (and already golden drops were beginning to seep through as he did so), then, after loosening it sufficiently, Grandfather pulled out the oak stopper with a sudden, decisive movement, thereby releasing a sun-coloured stream. Had it been water or, say, home-brewed beer, the stream would have arched sharply and struck the ground a long way off, but this liquid was thick and viscous, so that it drooped down under its own weight. It did not really flow, but fell into the vessel below, where it lay this way and that, in thick, transparent folds which only later spread out evenly.

I wonder why it was specifically this stream that arose in my memory and not simply the tub full of honey (which would also have made an impressive picture, of course)? Doubtless the reason was that in those days, owing to my tender years, I should not have been able to see into the tub. The stream, however, emerged at my height, on a level with my eyes.

I retrieved our tub from the neighbour, albeit without its bottom, stood it on the lawn in front of the house and everyone suddenly saw what a beauty she was.

People – former peasants – would come and place the palms of their hands against the tub and say: 'No. . . . Nobody makes them like this nowadays, not for a thousand roubles. It's the walls – they're so thin, just like paper.'

The walls, of course, were thicker than paper, they might have been as thick as a human hand. The thing was that the impressive size of the tub itself made the walls seem unusually thin.

'Nowadays you won't find a lime like that anywhere in the country either.'

'It isn't the lime that matters. The main thing is to season the wood. If they had hollowed it out from unseasoned wood, could it possibly have survived until now?'

'Right, and if you tried to dry it, it would crack on you. Again you'd end up without a tub.'

'That's not the point, mates. The thing is that everything in those days was done by hand, I reckon.'

'There's that, too – skilled hands. Where will you find them?'

'Ivan Vasilyevich is dead. Perhaps he could have done it.'

'You're right there – he's dead.'

And so our tub found itself standing on the green grass of the lawn, where it was something of a museum piece; but it was quickly put to good service. A young sapling planted in front of the house needs to be protected from goats, who will sink their teeth into anything; and so the bottomless, century-old limewood tub, so grey with age it was blue, was soon to be seen protectively encircling a young and tender little lime. The idea was to let them stay together for ever. Anyway, how could you take the tub away after five years or so, when the sapling would have grown a bit and spread out at the top? However, in reality things turned out differently. A drunken tractor-driver caught it with his wheel on a dark night and that was the end of the tub.

Nevertheless, whilst it was still in one piece, I managed to tell my children that, during my childhood, this very tub stood in our beekeeping hut, full of new honey.

Grandfather's beekeeping hut (which was also used as a winter apiary) was right there in the orchard, too; although it would be more accurate to say that the door of the hut opened on to the orchard, whereas the structure itself, which was timber made, full of the smell of wax and honey, dry and somehow lifeless, reposed within the yard. It was better like that, away from the wind, driving rains and buffeting blizzards. It would have been useless to cut a window through into the darkness of the yard, and that was the reason for the feeling of lifelessness which you always felt upon stepping out of the wide world into this cosy hut, lit as it was only by the light from the open door.

The winter apiary, that is the beekeeping hut in winter,

I do not remember. The bees wintered there and it was kept shut. The pure snow would pile up against the low door as high as the lintel with its small icon of St Vladimir, patron saint of bees; but in summer the empty frames which hung in bundles on the walls like strings of ring-shaped biscuits, the broad, flat knives, the sweet-smelling, delicate leaves of artificial foundation wax which would crackle gently when you pulled them apart, the weightless dead bees (a golden dust which is always present where bees are kept), the large wooden spoons used in summer to scrape away the growth which appears on the wood, these and many other different beekeeping utensils were there, recording the very first worldly impressions on the clean pages of my book of life, pages which were only just beginning to turn.

The object that is most clearly focused in my memory is the smoker. Even when it was cold and empty, just the same you squeezed the bellows and a puff of fragrant air would be expelled through the dark iron nozzle; and the edges around the hole in the nozzle were covered with a bumpy, black, greasy deposit. You put pieces of dry, white, rotten wood into the smoker and then start to squeeze and release the yellow leather bellows. At first only a hoarse noise, with nothing interesting to look at, emerges from the iron nozzle, along with some fine bits of ash remaining from the previous occasion. Then a bluish, yet still almost colourless stream of smoke appears. With every squeeze of the smoker this stream of smoke becomes a darker blue and thicker, until, when the pieces of rotten wood really catch, it turns into a kind of thick greenish milk. It goes straight and fast when first expelled from the smoker under pressure, but when it hits the air it begins to curl and form itself into an elaborate little cloud.

My father would hand me the smoker and take me to a hive. I could never get used to it. Every time I had that repulsive, gnawing feeling in the pit of my stomach which is called fear.

'Don't wave your arms about,' my father would say. 'If a bee crawls over you, don't touch it. It's when you touch it that it stings you. Leave it and it will crawl about a bit and fly away. It doesn't want to die for no reason any more than we do, you know.'

The smoker is in my hands. Father is walking ahead of me. Fear grips my heart more tightly at every step, but now the last step is behind me and there is a sense of relief. The psychology of fear does not vary with circumstances. Is there not the same feeling of relief when, for example, you pluck up courage and jump into cold water?

Father calmly removes the cover from the hive and places it on the grass. This reveals a piece of closely woven material so saturated with propolis that it has become as shiny as oilcloth. Father lifts up the corner of this material a little and I quickly aim the stream of smoke inside; but, just the same, like boiling water from a pot, the seething bees crowd out from under the material in the direction of the smoke. I keep up the hard work with the smoker. Now the material is taken right away. Beneath it are the yellow frames in rows and a moving mass of bees. Father would remove a frame and lift it up, shaking the swarm of bees that clung to it back into the hive. Half the bees would fall back and crawl away into the hive, but the other half would rise up into the air. Bees would be crawling over my hands. They crawl on my cheeks, too, and that tickles, they are on my neck, behind my ear and on my lip. I stand motionless, doing as Father taught me. Bees are crawling on his hands also. They get caught in his beard and, when this happens, buzz violently. Now that is dangerous. It is a sign of calamity, an alarm signal and a call for help. I see a bee arch its abdomen and sting Father's hand near a bulging blue vein. Father calmly plucks the bee from his hand and just as calmly pulls out the sting with his clumsy, rough fingers. Attached to the sting is a tiny piece of the bee's insides which have come away. At this same instant I too feel a burning sensation in my wrist, then in my neck. I am still holding my ground and do not throw down the smoker or run.

'They're angry,' says Father. 'Go along now, I'll carry on by myself. . . .'

Going up to a beehive with a smoker in your hand is nothing compared with the problem of calmly leaving it again. You must not run, shrieking and waving your arms, but take your time as you move from the sunny green orchard into the semi-darkness of the yard.

When the apiary stopped functioning, the beekeeping hut was turned into a general lumber-room, although various beekeeping utensils were left lying about in it. Amongst the items unrelated to beekeeping an old-fashioned gramophone was living out its days. This was a wonderful thing, as I now realize, especially on account of its beautiful horn, decorated in the Zhostovo style,[3] quite apart from its, let us say, sentimental value for me, since it was originally brought from the village of Karavaevo together with Stepanida Ivanovna's dowry.

I should like to buy one like it now, but where can you find one for sale, never mind the price?

I wonder where the horn could have got to? Its disappearance has left my memory without a trace. It was black, as if lacquered, and decorated all over with red, blue and green flowers. Then it was gone. Where did it go to? Did they simply throw it out? For that to happen it would have to have been dented first, its luxuriant flowery bell-end flattened ready to be discarded and disappear in the earth along with other remnants of human activity. Did the neighbours take it? If they had it still in one piece, I should have heard about it – anyway, of what use would it be to them without the gramophone? Most likely our village blacksmith, Nikita Kuzov, found a use for it at work.

But the gramophone itself – which comprised a polished (perhaps even mahogany) box with little columns at the corners, a turntable (to which was affixed a piece of thin green baize), a handle which was inserted at an angle into the hole at the side, whereupon it would catch hold of something and become harder and harder to wind, a small nickel-plated arm, shiny levers and pointers – this gramophone performed a very special service for me. Set up on the threshold of the beekeeping hut and aimed towards the orchard, it became a machine-gun which could mow down and decimate any army. The governor had gone wrong and when the spring was wound up the turntable would begin to spin uncontrollably and with gathering speed. The completely unchecked rate at which it spun finally caused the whole machine to vibrate and shake violently. The gramophone would jerk and thrash about, but the lines of White Guards (White Guards, of course, who else?) kept advancing, whilst I feverishly blazed away into Grandfather's orchard, into its green grasses, yellow flowers and one-time apiary, into that peaceful, kind-hearted paradise, a paradise already touched by the perdition that was to come to all.

So, someone had already managed (who knows when and how?) to implant into my young soul a thirst for blood and murder, and not ordinary murder, but mass murder from the barrel of a machine-gun, with people falling down row upon row and piling up in heaps. I could not get enough; the wildly spinning turntable, deprived of its governor, simply kept on going.

The Whites were coming, the turntable spun, but soon I needed more than just the shaking machine and I would help it out with my voice: 'Tra-ta-ta-ta-ta . . . tra-ta-ta-ta-ta. . . .'

Whilst this was happening, at which shoulder was there triumphant sniggering and at which was there suffering and tears?

5

IT WAS, HOWEVER, QUIET, PEACEFUL CREATIVITY THAT FIRST met me on earth.

When a train leaves the rails, providing it is heavy and its speed great enough, its momentum makes it hurtle straight on for a time before it begins to fall apart. With the train already flying into the abyss, into certain death, a child in, say, one of the middle carriages might remain asleep for a while in its berth; or perhaps it is playing or sucking its mother's breast. In a train that has come off the rails this extra time of 'well-being' lasts, probably, only seconds. If, on the other hand, a whole huge country comes off the rails, then, I should think, it may take years, if not decades, for it to hurtle into the abyss.

Somewhere else everything had happened, everything had been done to determine things for decades ahead, but in a little village lost amidst the green Vladimir countryside the crystal-clear river still ran through the flowering meadows, the loam, thick and fertile with manure, was still being loosened and turned by the plough, the village herd still dozed at midday, the carts creaked along under their load of wheatsheaves, the hens clucked and the sharp scythes rasped against the dewy grass. . . .

Yet now, speaking in this chapter about peaceful creativity, I do not mean our family's agricultural activities, although in itself there is nothing finer than to sow a seed or a grain and grow something that people find meaningful and useful. The point is that my grandfather, Aleksey Dmitrievich, had two factories.

There! Gasps throughout the auditorium! The seats are abuzz! Here and there, from this row, from that corner, remarks, not sympathetic remarks but shrill and gleeful ones, cut through the general noise: (He) 'What did I tell you!' (She) 'No, it was I who told you!' 'We bent over backwards for him, made such a fuss of him! He put Nicholas II on his finger – we forgave him.[4] He started protecting churches – we forgave him. He covered his wall with icons – we forgave him. He hobnobbed with émigrés in Paris – we forgave him. He did the same with the Patriarch and other holy Joes in Zagorsk – we forgave him. He subjected our life, our bright, happy life, to criticism in short stories, long stories, features – and we forgave him. He wrote the poem "Wolves" . . . now that surely makes it obvious we were ready to forgive him everything. We thought they were all casual slips, temporary delusions, but now everything's clear!'

It has indeed been a matter of importance for people of recent generations, over a number of decades, to single out the poverty of their social origins for special emphasis when writing books about themselves, about their childhood, or when composing other autobiographical pieces. For some reason poverty here is equated with cleanliness. 'A clean biography'; 'clean details on a form'; 'a clean past'. Cleanliness. If you come from a family of poor peasants – good. If your forbears were horseless (such people comprised, probably, no more than one per cent of the Russian peasantry) – wonderful. If they were cowless – superb.

Yet in doing this are we not creating a contrast between labour and cleanliness, as if the two were hostile, mutually exclusive concepts? After all, before you could acquire a horse (they could be bought at any market) or a cow, a pedigree bull or a stallion, before you could set up a windmill or a watermill, a forge or a saddler's business, before you could make shaft-bows or boil tar and wheel-grease, you needed money. And where did it come from? Money equals labour, as they taught us in school or, if not in school, then in college, in lectures on political economy. You might assume that a few of the peasants who bought a horse or even two, who kept bloodstock or became millers, first of all robbed someone on the highway or found some buried treasure. But not all of them! Is it not simpler to suppose that somewhere, sometime, somehow they worked harder than other people and that this led them to have more money than the rest?[5]

Has anyone tried to trace the particular circumstances that allowed one peasant farm to grow in strength and flourish, whilst another went on vegetating?

Further, if we go on saying 'the poorer, the better and cleaner', shall we not start contradicting common sense in a way that is obvious to everyone?

The horseless peasant could not have produced the thoroughbred Orlov trotter of which we are proud to this day and which even now earns us pure gold abroad. Nor could he have produced the Vladimir Bityug carthorse. The sheepless peasant could not have created the thoroughbred Romanov sheep. The cowless peasant could not have created those Russian and Vologda butters which had an unrivalled position on the world market. The wretched, poor, landless and almost landless peasants could not have come up with pure Russian apples such as the Antonovka, Grushovka Moskovskaya, Ukrainian Simirenko or Alma Ata Oporto, nor could they have produced the Vladimir cherry, Klimov cucumber, Rostov onion, Nezhin gherkin, Ryazan cabbage, Kuban wheat. You could go on for ever. . . .

The horseless, landless, wretched, poor peasants alone could not have flooded the world market with Russian oats, Russian sheepskins, Russian wax, Russian flax, Russian caviare, Russian crabs, Russian porcelain and cut glass, Russian pearls (Burmitsky pearls), Russian enamel or Russian silver. For some reason things made from Russian silver even today have a value ten times higher than other foreign silver. Take our famous eighty-four carat silver.

The horseless, cowless peasants could not of course have single-handedly won wars, nor could they have expanded the bounds of the state (which we all know covers a sixth of the world's surface). They would not have been able to organize expeditions right around the world or to ensure the flowering of art and science or the accumulation of vast material and spiritual wealth in the country.

Perhaps it is 'cleaner' and more noble to buy eggs in Poland, chickens in France, mutton in Argentina and wheat in Australia, Canada and the United States; perhaps it is better to sell Raphaels, Rembrandts and Titians rather than acquire them; perhaps it is better to demolish valuable works of architecture in the form of ancient churches than to build them; perhaps all that is 'cleaner' and better, but you must still admit that with horseless and cowless peasants alone Russia would have had neither military glory nor her wide expanses, nor Mendeleev, nor Pavlov, nor Tolstoy, nor Gogol, nor Pushkin, nor Tchaikovsky, nor the Tretyakov Gallery, nor the Hermitage, nor St Petersburg, nor Moscow, nor everything she successfully accumulated or created, whose remains we have been pulverizing now for over half a century and still have not managed to pulverize completely out of existence.

As far as money itself is concerned, just the same today too, some have more of it, some less. In Peredelkino not long ago a writer (a no-good writer, if the truth be known) built a ping-pong room at his dacha which, they say, came to twenty thousand, which is approximately what a collective-farm worker earns in our country over thirty years. I reckon both Grandfather's enterprises, with which I very nearly gave my audience a nasty fright, cost less than the ping-pong room and, what is more, unlike that room, they produced noble and useful items.

So, Grandfather had two factories. But I can calm my stunned and gasping audience down a little: let them not imagine factory chimneys, smoky shop-floors, clanking machinery, driving-belts (bearing in mind the level of technological development at that time), or the thump of

31

hammers, or any of that – what do they say? – Moloch. One of Grandfather's factories resembled in external appearance and size nothing more than an ordinary village bath-house and stood in the kitchen garden amidst the nettles and docks, separated only by a path from the blackcurrant bushes, raspberry canes and vegetable beds containing bumpy cucumbers and dill with its large stems and big seeds.

Water was poured into a copper cauldron set into the stove, after which dark-coloured bits and pieces of old honeycomb, light in weight compared with the water, were added. Not that it was exclusively tiny bits and pieces that were added but, nevertheless, all the honeycombs were broken up and mangled. They weighed very little and floated. I may be mistaken, but I seem to remember that, as the cauldron became warmer, the surface of this gently floating broken mass would coagulate and fuse together into a dark-brown crust resembling hills with bright yellow valleys or, if you prefer, lakes. Firewood was constantly put into the stove, the surface of the cauldron's contents would grow yet more uneven and swollen, until it finally burst at its weakest spot and boiling, seething water would rush out and flood the whole cauldron.

'It's a revolution! A revolution!' my elder brother, Nikolay, would cry out when this happened, and straight away he received a good clout on the back of the head from Grandfather.

Whether the boiling process lasted a long time or a short time, and what other apparatus was involved, I do not know. It should be possible now to read it up somewhere or locate a similar production line and take a look, but, you know, you would have to search and search. My selective memory obligingly provides me with a scoop: an old bucket fixed to a long handle. This scoop is dipped into the cauldron and then, shrouded in white steam, sails out in an arc through the air. At this point I would jump well out of the way because it might splash. I see in sharp focus the contents of the scoop, a soggy black mass, being poured into a wooden trough or, rather, into a rectangular hollow cut in a thick log and lined with a layer of clean, long-stemmed straw. They would wrap the straw around its liquid contents, as if swaddling them in it, and then weight it all down with a flat, heavy block of wood. Then they would put pressure on the block: not with their hands and feet, of course, but by means of a special mechanism, a press. There was a screw much thicker than the shaft of a cart fixed vertically above the trough and a nut that looked like a small barrel and which, when turned, moved up and down the screw. There were sockets in this barrel-like nut and into these sockets two poles – actual shafts from a cart, this time – would be inserted. Two people (Grandfather and Father, or my father and brother) would walk round in a circle pushing the poles, which then turned the nut. The nut descended and pressed down on the block and the block pressed on the straw and on the soggy mass wrapped up in it. As a result of this pressure a hot black stream, filtered by the straw, flowed out through the aperture provided.

I also ran round the circle whilst this was going on, pretending to help by holding one of the poles, but in order to reach it I had to lift up my little arms. The poles turned two or three times without effort or effect before the press touched the block and began to exert pressure and, moving freely, they spun like a merry-go-round. Perhaps it is on account of this merry-go-round that I remember so distinctly those oak poles with their kinks, smooth bumps and two remaining patches of bark which had, like the poles as a whole, become greasy and polished.

When the straw that had been squeezed out under the press was tossed out of the trough and thrown to one side, it gave off hot steam. After pressing, it looked like a small children's mattress.

The stream emerging from the press ran into another copper cauldron, one-third full of cold, clean water. The flow of liquid was black, but also in its own way clean. Just as earlier, at the start of the process, the light, dry bits of honeycomb had floated in the cauldron which had been set into the stove, so here too that item which constituted the 'factory's' purpose floated up and accumulated on the surface of the water. It was magical to dip my finger into that black mass (still hot, but evidently my skin was able to bear it) and then pull it out as quickly as possible along with the bright, shiny yellow thimble that had instantly appeared upon it. The transformation of black into yellow and the sensation in my finger itself as the hot substance gave it a sudden sharp burn, these things made a different impression on me from the rest of the world. I once saw my brother Victor, who was older than I and more mischievous and boisterous, dip his whole hand in as far as the wrist and end up with a yellow waxen glove. True, it could not be removed whole from his hand and had to be broken off. Oh yes, I remember now, in order to take the thimble off whole, you had to dip your finger into cold water before putting it into the hot wax.

The black fluid in the cauldron would cool and gradually become yellow itself, turning into a large cake of pure wax. Thanks to its being in water, the cake was easily taken out of the cauldron, the thin layer of brownish scum with bubbles in it was removed from the top with a sharp scraper and then it was placed on the scales.

A long shaving would curl up and occasionally break as you watched the movement of the scraper. At the same time the glossy surface of the wax, with scraper marks in it, would be revealed. The denser the surface and the fewer greenish bubbles of air in it, the better the wax – in other words, the more successful the wax-making had been.

Father would take a large bent nail and trace figures and letters on the cake, say, 2 pds 4 pnds. That would be two poods, four pounds of finished product.[6]

When a few cakes were ready, Father would load them on the cart, cover them over with hay, clover or fresh grass and take them off to Vladimir. When he returned there would be big bast sacks on the cart, full of our 'raw material' – old, empty honeycombs, their honey removed either by centrifugal force or by heating in a stove. The combs, which were already broken up into small pieces, were tipped out into the corner of the shed which was attached to our wax-maker's place. There they lay in a dark brown heap, giving off a faint but distinct smell. When the heap was nearly used up we would find a great variety of small objects on the floor beneath it. Every load of empty combs promised new finds, although how they got there is not clear. There was a glass stopper, a brass doorknob, nails and buttons, horse brasses, bells and once even a real revolver turned up. The revolver had a cylinder with cartridges in it, though it was not a Nagant, as I now realize, but some ancient model. More often than not (and this was actually the most interesting part), we found small change – silver and bronze coins. You must bear in mind that a twenty-copeck coin was still a twenty-copeck coin then and that it really was made of silver. It was not just a nondescript bit of metal.

I do not know where Father found the old combs. I do not believe he went round villages and hamlets buying them up from the beekeepers. It would be simpler to suppose that there was in Vladimir, as we would say now, an official collection point, where the population would take the empty combs and which would be frequented by people who practised the same trade as my father and grandfather. It could be that they gave Father the old combs in exchange for the pure wax, settling the difference in value with real money. That, however, is only a supposition. One cannot rule out the possibility that three bags of old combs could be bought in those days at the market just as simply as three sacks of birchwood charcoal, a sack of dried Caspian roach, a horse, a cart, a tarantass, a sleigh, a small sledge, a shaft-bow, roofing iron, timber, boards, bricks, shingles, oats, linseed oil, curried sheepskins, bast and bast matting, leatherware, raw leather, tar, rope, oakum and moss, wool and curried cowhide, box calf and canvas, joiner's glue, drying oil and wax. . . .

Thinking of these large sacks full of empty honeycombs – our raw material – I remember Grandfather's touching fussiness and, at the same time, strictness when we sat drinking tea with honey and he would not allow us to spit carelessly aside or throw away the little balls of wax that we came across, even though they had been sucked at, rolled around in our mouths and chewed up. Instead, we had to make a neat little heap of them in a saucer. There would scarcely be many of them, but they too would be added to the heap of old combs, tossed into the cauldron, melted down and turned into a few grammes of finished product.

The wax produced in our wax-maker's place was probably used for the church candles which would blaze warmly during the Liturgy and nocturnal services, but it was also and more often used for making those translucent sheets of 'artificial foundation wax' which would come apart with a faint crackle and which were so indispensable to every beekeeper. This type of wax was called artificial not because it was some form of substitute, ersatz or plastic, but because part of the work was done artificially for the bees beforehand: the six-sided cells for the combs were already stamped out on the wax sheets and the bees had simply to work at them, build them up, fill them with honey and seal them.

Wax was made whilst the weather was warm and so, apart from unexpected finds amongst the spent combs (such as silver coins), apart from the yellow cakes of wax, pot-bellied weights and straw surrounded by a sweet-smelling mist, apart from the boiling cauldron full of combs and the pinching, hot, yellow thimbles of wax on my finger, our wax-maker's is associated in my mind with the brilliant summer sun, blue sky and cool grass.

Finally, I must not forget the two logs that lay in the grass beneath those blue skies. They were short, but with a diameter, I should think, equal to my height at the time. Evidently the intention was to increase productivity: those logs could only have been put by to make new troughs for the wax-maker's place; but there they were, left mouldering in the grass until, half rotten, they were sawn up and chopped into firewood. The train, you see, had long since left the track, life was going on simply under its own momentum, but the momentum itself was shuddering to a halt. . . .

. . . The only workman at our wax-maker's, apart from Grandfather himself, was my father. His adolescent sons, Nikolay and Victor, helped him, but I only interfered and got in everyone's way; and, what is more, they had other things to do and most likely could devote to it only those inconvenient moments that remained after the harrowing, sowing, haymaking and reaping were done, the sheaves gathered in, the threshing and ploughing completed and the potatoes lifted. . . .

Grandfather's other enterprise was also seasonal, being active from spring until the autumn. Extra hands were certainly needed there. First of all it required a skilled craftsman, an expert; secondly, we would simply never have managed on our own. So, apart from our permanent expert, Ondrey[7] Ivanych (I cannot resist spelling his name as I knew it in childhood), every summer we hired two assistants for him who pushed wheelbarrows full of sand and clay over narrow pathways made of planks. They would put the green bricks ready for firing, as well as those already fired, beneath tentlike awnings with shingled roofs.

Yes, and here is another important item for the form: hired labour. They tried to impress the idea on us so hard and bamboozled us with it so much that we actually began to believe that hiring people for any type of work was virtually a crime; but of course it is the most natural activity ever known to man. Do our country people not hire, let us say, a shepherd for the whole season even now? Take our neighbour, Ksenia Ivanovna. A short time ago she hired some men and they cleaned and repaired her well for her. Yes, you will say, but what about appropriation of another's labour, what about surplus value? . . . But with collective farms paying their people in money these days, do not all those tractor-drivers, operators of combine harvesters and other machinery, milkmaids and all the other farm workers to the last man and woman, do they really not represent hired labour? And does our state, in hiring its workers, really make sure that the amount of work they do is proportional to their wages? Does not the state itself appropriate a huge amount of so-called surplus value? That is why the state fought against petty 'exploiters', so it could become the one and only colossal exploiter itself.

A brick in human civilization is the same as a cell of vegetable or animal tissue in nature. Nature, as is known, will not put up with monotony and standardization; yet all her prodigious variety is founded on a more or less standard basic material – the cell. In the same way, what can be more standard or uninspiring than an ordinary brick? Nevertheless, all kinds of temples and palaces spring up on this earth, as well as walls around churches, watch-towers, factory buildings and chapels, apartment blocks and stations. These structures may hug the ground, or they may rise up like a gushing stream or hang in the air as delicate and joyful as flowers, or again, they may form a looming, sombre mass, but it is all done out of virtually identical little bricks.

The collective farm to which our village belongs has had a succession of chairmen. I recall a conversation about bricks I had with one of them. This chairman cherished a dream of demolishing the church that stood in the centre of the village.

'What a cowshed we could put up with those bricks! And there'd be some left over for a pigsty – for the supports at least. Ah!'

'But just think it through,' I urged him. 'Would it be any cheaper? It costs money to knock the church down, too, you know. Wouldn't it be easier to bring a load of bricks ready for use?'

'Where would you find them?'

'Bricks?'

'Yes, of course. In Stavrovo there was a brickyard – they closed it down. . . . And anyway, the bricks were no good. They would soak right through when it rained. Do proper bricks do that? They were all misshapen, bulging somehow, and if you knocked one against your knee it would fall to pieces. Or it would break up into layers, like a piecrust made of flaky pastry. I know for a fact that the old sort couldn't be smashed with a sledgehammer. They were like flint – you could probably start a fire with them. And they were cheaper than wood – just clay and water. Well, sand too. I see in your area (this chairman, like all his predecessors and successors, was sent to us from somewhere in town) people liked brick houses. Look at Stavrovo, Yarmonino, Rozhdestveno, Eltesunovo, Cherkutino – they're just full of brick houses! And they are still there. Nothing's happened to them.'

'Isn't there supposed to be a brickyard near Undol?'

'It's lousy. Perhaps just a bit better than the one at Stavrovo. Then of course all the collective farms in the region use it. You'd be queueing for weeks. True, there is a brickyard the other side of Vladimir which makes silica bricks. They're grey, as you probably know. Now all the houses over there are grey.'

'Do you really have to go to Vladimir and even farther away for bricks?'

'That's just it. If we could demolish the church . . . '

'In the Ukraine and north Kazakhstan, when they want to put a house up in a village, they make their building materials on site. Admittedly they use adobe bricks rather than ordinary ones, but you have to mix, mould and dry them too. I reckon it is even harder to make an adobe brick than an ordinary clay one.'

'What are you getting at?'

'This. Is it so impossible for your collective farm to set up a brickyard of its own? First, it would satisfy its own needs, then, in order to justify the expenditure, you could . . . well, I reckon a bit of profit would not be so bad.'

'Not bad? It would be very good!'

'So, what's the problem?'

'I don't really know, except that I've never come across a single collective-farm brickyard anywhere. Perhaps they exist somewhere, but I've never seen one in our area.'

'Ah, but did you know that Alepino had its own brickyard until comparatively recently?'

'There were a great many things until recently,' the chairman replied unenthusiastically to my piece of news. 'Some people were saying that there used to be twenty watermills working away on the Koloksha, and that's not much of a river. A regular cascade! But now if you want a sack of flour ground, there's not a single mill to do it, except in the regional centre. . . . So, did Alepino actually have its own brickyard? Where was it, then?'

'You go via Glafira's cattle-track to the river, then, after the detached houses and gardens have ended but before the hill begins, well, immediately after the present school, to the left of it, beyond the semidetached prefabricated house . . . in the past, you know, neither the school, nor that house, nor anything else was there. . . . Well, most likely you know there's a sizeable pit there, like a quarry, only not deep, about a metre and a half . . . it's all covered over with green grass now. . . . You would not even notice it. . . . You would think that the land for some reason had just sunk a bit, but that's where the brickyard was. . . .'

Two smells – one of wax, the other of freshly mixed clay – stand out amongst the intermingled smells of my childhood: those of straw, honey, raspberries, smoke from the stove (before you can carry a smouldering log across the kitchen and throw it out on to the snow, it fills the whole house with fumes), the smell of the samovar being stoked (more smoke), of milk fresh from the cow, of horses (and the yard in general), of jasmin and lilac (which grew in front of the house), of damask violets and lilies of the valley (my sisters loved them and kept them in their room), of hot flat cakes, warm loaves, vegetable (linseed) oil, rye, naphthalene (when we played hide-and-seek we would get into the big wardrobe and sit there with the clothes hanging around us), of sheepskins, apples, the smoker, of a bonfire in the woods, of wild strawberries, young olives, summer rain (in reality, the smell of earth and nettles), of paraffin (in the lamps) . . . there's plenty more. And then there are those two distinct childhood smells – molten wax and clay freshly mixed in a box.

Under the pressure of a foot in a boot the sharp spade would cut easily into the ground and take out a spadeful. The clay would come out in rich, shiny lumps. It seemed surprising that clear drops did not appear on the cut edge, as happens when you slice into fresh fatty cheese. The clay was a bold, dark red, heavy and cool, as you could tell if you put a freshly cut spadeful to your cheek.

The clay was taken in a wheelbarrow along a pathway made of boards (one plank wide) to a sizeable but shallow wooden box, where it was mixed together with clean sand from the river. At the same time water was added. The water was kept in a small pond which would fill up in spring, more or less survive thanks to the summer rains but then practically dry up by the autumn, although the rains would start again then anyway. There was a white willow with dense foliage and a crown that grew out over the water and prevented the sun from reaching it, and this helped the pond not to evaporate in the summer heat. The shadow of the willow was large enough to cover the entire surface of the water. In spring the pond would teem with tadpoles and in summer, naturally, with frogs. The hollow that is there now fills with water as the snow melts but very quickly dries up, because the willow is no longer there. Moreover, in those days, quite possibly they made the pond deeper each year, if only a little, and looked after it. You cannot make bricks without water.

Ondrey Ivanych worked covered in clay (bits of bright-red clay stuck to his black beard); and his bench was covered in clay too. There was nothing special about his bench, it was like an ordinary table, and as far as his method of work was concerned. . . . The same method was used by ice-cream ladies before the war: they would place a wafer at the bottom of a shallow cylinder, fill the cylinder with ice-cream, put another wafer on top and then press a lever and the ice-cream would, so to speak, pop up out of its nest ready to be taken and eaten.

Only here the hole in the bench was not round, but rectangular and the correct size for the future brick. Instead of a wafer Ondrey Ivanych would put a thin, sturdy, brick-sized piece of metal at the bottom of the hole and then pack in clay of the necessary mix on top of it. Next, he would remove the superfluous clay, smooth it off with a wooden float, press on a pedal with his foot and the brick, together with the piece of metal, would come up out of its nest. Ondrey Ivanych would take it and carefully place it on its side on a smooth board. The brick is ready. It has only to dry out in the shade beneath the awning, where there is a light breeze, after which it is fired in a special kiln.

Whilst the brick is drying in the wind you can creep up and, if you are quick, press your palm on it. I wonder, amongst all those villages and all those houses with their foundations and stove chimneys, has even one of my palmprints survived?

The kiln was not fired frequently, perhaps two or three times every summer. Ondrey Ivanych had to make a sufficient quantity of bricks to fill it each time. It would take . . . I do not know how many, and there is no one to ask now, but I dare say a few thousand bricks. Actually, bricks were reckoned and sold in hundreds. You would say 'fifteen hundred', not 'one and a half thousand'. Ondrey Ivanych would climb into the kiln and the green bricks would be handed in for him to stack in the correct way. The vast interior of the kiln would slowly fill up. From the outside the kiln resembled a small house or, more accurately, barn. It had a conical shingled roof, open at the apex. Above this opening was suspended a smaller cone like a kind of cowl. The smoke would emerge from the opening, build up beneath the cowl, swirl up above it and trickle out in all directions from under the edges. Down below, the kiln had a number of low, vaulted furnaces which would be filled up with dry firewood. Everyone – Ondrey Ivanych, Grandfather, Father – would fuss nervously around the kiln. Clearly the firing of the bricks was an important operation, it could be successful or less successful and upon it depended, as they would say now, the quality of the finished product.

The finished product, the fired, tough, resonant bricks, were stacked beneath a long awning on short posts with a gable roof covered with shingles. The shingles, dark with age, shone in the sun and shimmered on clear moonlit nights like fine old silver.

Green grass touched with the gold of dandelions, the bright red of the clay and bricks and the dark silver of the wooden buildings – such was the range of colours found in that spot then. Oh, add to it the sparkling mirror of the pond and Ondrey Ivanych's gypsy-black beard.

I do not know the nature of the relations that existed between the master brickmaker, Ondrey Ivanych, one of our ordinary Alepino folk who had simply learnt to make bricks, and my grandfather, the owner of the factory, the capitalist. What was he paid for his labour? What was his working day? What was the cost of the finished product? What was the level of productivity at the factory? What was the net profit?

I know only that Aleksey Dmitrievich spent every winter's evening during the last years of his life, when the factory, naturally, was no longer working (he died in 1933), sitting at Ondrey Ivanych's. He would finish drinking his tea, put on his coat, take his stick and off he would go. 'I'll just sit awhile with Ondrey Ivanych,' he would tell everyone at home, and then he would sit with him till late. My grandfather was very religious, there was no question of any draughts or cards. So these two old men, these two opponents, these two implacable class enemies – the capitalist, Aleksey Mitrich, and his hired craftsman,

Ondrey Ivanych – would spend the long winter evenings in unhurried conversations. What would they talk about? I imagine they recalled the brickyard together.

Our little brickyard died somehow suddenly. Somewhere up there they turned a stopcock and the pulse of life ceased forthwith, even though the long awning where the bricks had been stored and the kiln with its conical roof and cowl remained standing for long afterwards. It all became part of the collective farm, but not a single brick was ever produced again. The remnants of the original bricks were left beneath the awning and, strangely, were not sold at all. Most likely no one in those days had a mind to build anything out of bricks. After all, the stopcock had been turned not only on a small brickyard and wax-maker's but on the entire surging, living pulse of life.

Nevertheless, as the years passed, little by little the quantity of bricks beneath the awning diminished (evidently they were needed to repair stoves). In the end there remained only broken fragments and crumbled brick. The white willow over the pond disappeared and the pond itself finally dried up completely. The wooden buildings somehow wasted away by themselves. It was as if everything around was melting, dissolving in the blue country air. Finally it all melted and dissolved to such an extent that not a rotten shingle, rusty nail or fragment of brick remained. Only the hollow where the kiln was, plus a fair-sized depression in the surrounding earth (now with a dense covering of short green grass) still indicate the spot where the skilful hands of Ondrey Ivanych fashioned tough, resonant, ten-pound Russian bricks from which were constructed churches and bell-towers, cemetery walls and barns, peasant houses, chapels, the foundations of wooden houses and Russian stoves.

However, after gulping down Grandfather's brickyard, history gave a couple of belches.

On the first occasion I was a student. I came home for the holidays to find my father, Aleksey Alekseevich, who was already getting on and almost too old for work on the collective farm, engaged in a strange activity. He was examining a large number of blueprints which he had spread out over the whole table. The scene struck me as very funny. I had already been through Technical College; I knew what a blueprint was and what the phrase 'to read a blueprint' meant. I was also aware that Father could not read blueprints any more than I could read, say, Arabic.

The mystery was soon explained. At that time a nationwide campaign was being got up (or, more accurately, sent down from on high) in connection with the proposal to build 'agritowns' – a ridiculous idea with which Khrushchev managed to distract Stalin for a time. There was a sudden need for bricks. Standard designs for the erection of small but efficient brickworks were distributed around the collective farms. In our farm they suddenly remembered that Aleksey Alekseevich must know at least something about brickmaking. He was put in charge of building the new brickyard.

I do not know what Father saw in the blueprints, but in actual fact there appeared (not in the original place, but in a ravine where there was plenty of clay) two awnings exactly similar to the earlier ones. I do not think they materialized there from the blueprints; most likely they emerged from Aleksey Alekseevich's memory.

They never got as far as building the kiln, let alone making bricks. They decided that the idea of setting up 'agritowns' was no good and dropped it. Just as before, the awnings added variety to the landscape for a while but then gradually disappeared, leaving no more trace than their predecessors, the only difference being that their time on earth had passed to no effect. From beneath their dry, cool canopy not a single brick emerged into the world.

The second splashback happened not long ago at all. The powers that be somehow found out that Alepino stands on superb clay. A mobile drilling machine immediately arrived in the village and geological prospectors began to examine the land in our area, taking samples here, there and everywhere, on the higher land as well as on the sides of the ravines; and, although a complete, cold, deathly indifference had long since permeated the hearts and souls of Alepino's inhabitants, no matter what else might be done to their land, however more it might be spoilt and tormented, its greenery ripped away by bulldozers, its even meadows churned up by tractor tracks, the sides of the ravines and the edges of the forest mutilated with piles of rotting potatoes, the forest filled with rubbish, the meadows allowed to turn into tussocks and bogs – although by then all that was looked upon in Alepino (as in every other Russian village) with a horrifying, deathly indifference, nevertheless a few inhabitants of the village felt distressed. 'That's it. We will be in the middle of one great clay-pit. There you are, they've taken a liking to our clay. So much for our hills and ravines. The whole area will be stripped bare and dug up.'

The prospectors' efforts led them to approximately the following conclusion. Yes, the clay was superb, but there was only a thin layer of it and the deposits were small. Of course those deposits would last an artisan with a single spade for up to two hundred years, but the state would exploit them on such a scale that they would run out very quickly and therefore there was no point in even starting the process.

After that the geologists had a good drink and set off back to town. However, their attempts to leave our boundaries were not completely successful. The drilling machine, driven by a drunken operator, toppled over into the ditch at the side of the road near Shunovo and lay there on its side for quite some time, eliciting sighs of relief from the locals: 'The calamity missed us, the state doesn't need our Alepino clay. . . .'

6

AT THE END OF AUGUST THE GILDING OF SUNLIGHT ON THE
fields, meadows and coppices is neither blinding nor
oppressively hot, but gentle and pleasant. The clouds are
more than usually swollen and rounded, and they are so
white that they seem to be lit both inside and out. The
haymaking is long since finished, the rye has been gathered
in from the fields; the peas, too. Only the oats and
buckwheat still await their turn and for the time being
continue to present an alluring spectacle to the flocks of
cranes as they fatten themselves in readiness for their
distant migration.

On the evening before a journey Father would take a
bucket full of wheel-grease and busy himself about the
cart. Each corner had to be raised in turn, so that the
wheel hung helplessly above the ground and turned freely
at the touch of a hand. A light tap (with the butt of an
axe) and the square iron linchpin would jump out of the
black, grease-bound axle. Father's hands would grasp the
rim of the wheel and, with a rocking movement to left
and right as if he were trying to steer, wrench it from the
axle and put it to one side on the grass. He would take a
flat little wooden trowel and scoop up some of the grease
in the bucket. The grease would appear thick and black,
although a thin layer of it would be brown. Father would
put a generous coating of grease evenly around the axle
and then push the heavy wheel back into place. The
linchpin was replaced next. Then he would lower that
corner of the cart and begin to lift another (with the help

of a shaft-bow and pole).

A little dog who has sensed that his master is about to go out for a walk jumps for joy, fusses impatiently about him and even whines in anticipation. I think that as a four-year-old I must have behaved in exactly the same way towards my father and the cart. Anyway, there was one occasion when, apart from the general sense that something was about to happen, apart from the self-evident preparations for a journey, everyone at home knew and was talking about the fact that the next day was the Feast of the Assumption and we were to go visiting in Karavaevo. My mother was going to comb my hair and dress me up in a new pair of trousers which reached to my knees. There would be socks and sandals and a loose-fitting white shirt. A piece of elastic had been threaded around the bottom edge of the shirt, which came down over the top of my trousers. On my head would be a little white panama hat and around my neck, under my shirt collar, a big wine-coloured bow. That is how I am in the 'Karavaevo photograph', which still exists. Next to me is my sister, Marusya, still a girl of about ten. She is six years older than I. So, I was four. She is holding some flowers in her hand, rudbeckias, and I have a little horse with four wheels bought at the local fair. The fact that both my shirt and the horse were white was the cause of real disappointment to me, as the toy did not come out in the picture. I clearly remember that feeling of disappointment when I first looked at the photograph at the time; or perhaps I should even say surprise. What's happened? My horse was there, I know it, my beautiful toy was there. . . .

The other circumstances surrounding that photograph have slipped my memory.

I do, though, have another three or four fragmented recollections of the trip to Karavaevo. Take those rudbeckias. For some reason they did not grow them in Alepino, but there, in Karavaevo, the front garden was full of them, it was like one huge bouquet. At the same time I do not recall the first thing about the house to which the garden belonged, not the porch, or the windows, or the gates. I remember only dimly, in brownish tones, the bearded face of Grandfather, Ivan Mikhaylovich – this was my mother, Stepanida Ivanovna's, father – so that it is not impossible that my recollection of him has been influenced by a later portrait (in oils) which was brought to Alepino in the 1930s, along with some other goods and chattels, when the Karavaevo house was nearing its end.

In the dense blue twilight of my memory a glassy smooth stream of water is flowing down a broad mill-race of sloping planks. The wooden mill-wheel slowly revolves amidst the trickling waters and hairlike greenery of the algae. The actual river and mill have remained somewhere merely in the vicinity of the mill-race and mill-wheel. They have been left out in the dark, having failed, so to speak, to be found by the lens and included in the shot.

Strictly speaking, only one shot has turned out to be exactly in focus, beautifully lit and fixed in my memory with the best possible exposure. I even see it as a kind of symbol of that special day, of Karavaevo as it used to be, of the fair and that particular visit of ours. The shot is of a new white sieve full of large, golden, translucent grapes.

The grapes without a doubt were bought at the fair. I would guess that such grapes were sold along with the sieves in which they were already packed. That is how it was: you bought not a pound or ten pounds of grapes but a sieve of them. They would not have to be weighed or handled more than necessary and so would not be damaged. The sieves themselves were probably very cheap but, if they were any good at all, you could always find a use for a new sieve somewhere at home.

The road to Karavaevo – the overall impression, if not the details – I recall more vividly and at greater length. The twenty versts in a squeaky cart pulled at an unhurried pace by our horse, Golubchik (encouraged by an even less hurried Aleksey Alekseevich, my father), took at least five hours. For five hours the gold-green, blue-white month of August processed slowly past us on both sides of the cart (as well as above and all about). The overall impression was of blue hills, with occasionally a pretty white bell-tower, dark wooded islands amidst the yellow flatness of the fields (empty by that time of the year) and the horizon on all sides, the horizon at the rim of the round, slightly concave expanse that was the wide world.

Drift on, drift on, wide world of my birth, drift on past the gaze of that fair-haired four-year-old, fill his soul to the brim, enough for a whole lifetime!

The overall impression may have been blue hills and little white churches, but in close-up and sharp focus I recall the soft clover in the cart which we sat on and the clusters of false spiraea which grew right next to the track, so that if you hung your legs over the side of the cart, the false spiraea and the stems of other grasses would brush against them and spots of black wheel-grease would be sure to end up on your skin near your knees: the carts that had passed that way before us had caught the grass with their axles. It was terribly difficult, even painful, to remove those marks, because the grease made the tiny downy hairs on your legs stick together.

The horse walked onward and at every step the structure of the major muscles moving beneath his skin caused deep, branched lines, like pitchforks, to become visible on his powerful brown haunches as they strained and relaxed in turn.

Now, from time to time Father would spy something unseen by us in the fields and begin to wave his whip about high in the air. Big grey birds would suddenly sail up in the distance. Hitherto they had been indistinguishable from the field and invisible to a child's inexperienced eye. They did not go far and certainly did not form themselves into the well-known wedgelike pattern typical of cranes. They simply flew off a little way in a loose flock, almost touching the panicles of the oats with their wings. Then they would lower their long, lanky legs and settle down in the field again. For a long time afterwards I would still be able to make out their watchful heads above the oats.

But why Assumption Day and why Karavaevo?

We went on Assumption Day because the church festival in Karavaevo used to be on that day as well as the fair and, moreover, Stepanida Ivanovna was from that village. Our father, Aleksey Alekseevich, was going to visit his parents-in-law. His father-in-law, Ivan Mikhaylovich Cheburov, an old man with a broad beard (my memory of whom over the years has become associated with the brown tones of the old portrait), kept a watermill in Karavaevo, on the River Peksha. He had four sons and two daughters. One of these was Stesha.[8]

My father, Aleksey Alekseevich Soloukhin, was originally married to Tatyana, but she died very young, leaving two children – Kostya and Shura, my elder half-brother and half-sister.

It is not known at what point and in what circumstances the twenty-seven-year-old widower began to notice Stesha. Perhaps he used to visit the mill and saw her there. Perhaps he saw her at one of the Assumption fairs. Anyway, matchmakers were sent. The broad-bearded miller (I should mention that he was blind by then) was lying on the Russian stove. Without getting down from the stove, he listened attentively to the unfamiliar voices and asked what was going on in the house.

'Well now, matchmakers have come. From somewhere called Alepino. Never heard of it . . .'

'Who are they?'

'Some people with the name of Soloukhin, apparently.'

'I know them. They're good folk. They can have her.'

Stesha was seventeen at the time.[9]

My mother told me more about Karavaevo than I know from these partial recollections of going there on Assumption Day at the beginning of my life. It was a big, prosperous village with a market, situated on the high bank of the shining River Peksha, a good river for fishing. On the other side of the river there were brightly coloured water-meadows. It was whilst she was gathering flowers in these meadows as a young girl that Stesha found two snow-white narcissi amongst the wild meadow grasses. They had drifted there from some other world.

The village on the high bank of the river was dominated by two beautiful white churches and a bell-tower. On the evening of the Day of the Holy Trinity the young men and girls danced round in a circle, perhaps three hundred people at a time. The girls would all be in long white dresses, their heads garlanded with cornflowers and globe-flowers. You can just imagine it. The Peksha teemed with fish. Once some country lads brought a pike to the miller (to sell or as a gift?) which they had caught with a drag-net, and it very nearly stretched all the way across the round table in the sitting-room of the Cheburov house.

The Alepino Soloukhins were lean, with black hair and straight noses. The Karavaevo Cheburovs were fair-haired, with wide noses and round faces and a tendency to put on weight. According to Bunin, old Russia was black and white. Boyarynya Morozova, Natasha Rostova and Tatyana Larina were on one side, with Olga Larina, Chaliapin and Esenin on the other.

In our family these two Russias mixed and merged; but still, both the one and the other were equally old Russia.

I dropped into Karavaevo during my journey on foot along the Vladimir by-roads in 1956; but at that time personal themes struck me as out of place in that sort of book and the pages of *Vladimir By-Roads* do not contain even a hint of them. Yet the fact is that I spent the night in Karavaevo and visited the spot where the Cheburov house and mill had been.

One thing has consistently been the case: the small villages have generally preserved their neat, cosy, pre-revolutionary, pre-collectivization look the longest. The large villages with their defunct churches, small shops, tea-houses, inns, two-storey buildings and apple orchards all quickly display signs of devastation, neglect and mismanagement. The bigger, more prosperous, beautiful and clean the town in the past, the more obvious are the signs today.[10] The village of Karavaevo had not escaped this fate.

I spent the night, as I recall, in a small cottage belonging to an elderly lady who lived on her own. She talked to me about Karavaevo the whole evening: what a green, clean, busy village it had been, what haymaking there used to be beyond the Peksha, how many fish there had been in the river, how beautiful the churches had been and what fairs had filled the air with their clamour on Assumption Day.

'Now then, I have heard that people called Cheburov used to live here . . .'

'Of course! They had a watermill on the Peksha. If you go there tomorrow you will see where the dam was. Nothing else is left, but you can see where the dam was. It was a good mill and beneficial to the river.'

'And the house?'

'It was nearby, on raised ground, in an open space away from the village. It was a fine big house.'

'Well, do you remember the Cheburovs, then?'

'Yes. Ivan Mikhaylovich is long since dead. He died in good time.'

'What do you mean, in good time?'

'Well, before collectivization. But Vasilisa I don't know about. You know their daughter, Stesha, got married and went to Olepino.[11] It's possible that Vasilisa lived out her last days with her in Olepino. Everything's gone to ruin here, there's no house and no mill. But how things are with the people in Olepino now, I can't say. . . .'

. . . There were no rudbeckias there, not in a single front garden (never mind that they would not have been out by that time of year), nor indeed were there any front gardens, or any grapes in sieves. I had a walk around the run-down, half-ruined village and went up to the churches. In one of them a treacle factory had been put up in a rush of enthusiasm and a black iron chimney had been fixed to the white wall; but now of course there was no question of any treacle. Everything was empty and dead. The other church had been knocked down. Its earthly remains had been pushed down the sheer drop to the river with a bulldozer; the whole of the steep bank was littered with pink and white rubble which stretched from the elevated site where the church had stood, down as far as the water which was black and poisonous now (thanks to the Kolchugino factories).

Beneath the church there used to be a crypt, the last resting-place of the Kuzmin-Karavaevs, Apraksins, Golitsyns and Vorontsovs. Stepanida Ivanovna told me that they took her to the crypt when she was young and that she had even wanted to touch a funeral ribbon, but it had crumbled to pieces when she tried. Later (see *Vladimir By-Roads*), the crypt was torn apart (when they were looking for Field-Marshal Vorontsov's sabre). All the bones were thrown out and the children ended up playing football with the Field-Marshal's skull.

An empty space had been left on the site of the Cheburovs' house. Beds of nettles were growing there, but even they were dying of age by then. I stood awhile near the nettles, trying to summon up some hazy memory of the house and of Grandfather, Ivan Mikhaylovich, but nothing came to mind apart from the rudbeckias and a sieve of grapes – oh, and a brownish portrait of an old man with a broad beard and wide nose.

You may wonder why I should be interested in that old man; or in the nettles and the defunct house and mill. Well, for some reason, by a twist of fate, I take after my mother's family and resemble specifically that old man.

One summer (really quite recently) I and my two elder sisters, Katyusha and Tonya, met up in Alepino and lived there together for a while. We spent July and August without taxing ourselves. The nights became noticeably darker and more starry. The evenings drew in. Still, by the end of the day you had had enough time to do all the work, reading and walking you wanted, so that you really had nothing much left to do in the evenings. Well I might, for example, go on shuffling away with my sheets of paper, but they (my sisters) had no cares, no worries, nor anything to do, so they started to play cards. All worthwhile games, though, are designed for three or four players or more. You resist as long as you can and then sit down to play with them: all right, then, let's have the spades, clubs, aces and queens. It became a habit.

Suddenly Katyusha says: 'We've forgotten, you know, tomorrow's Assumption Day. We're going visiting in Karavaevo.'

'Of course,' Tonya joined in, 'Pa's already greased the wheels. Tomorrow he'll harness Golubchik, throw some fresh clover into the cart and we'll be off. They said the weather's going to be fine and dry tomorrow, so the fair won't be rained off.'

(It was 1969, Aleksey Alekseevich had been lying in the ground for twelve years already and Stepanida Ivanovna for two. The cart and Golubchik had been gone for decades. Not a stone of the Cheburov house had been left standing and there was no question of any fair, but – imagine that – the memories came flooding back as we played cards on that August evening, the eve of the Feast of the Assumption.)

'You know, it was another planet. Amazing, we seem to be the same people, but it's like living on another planet. . . . Another thing I remember is that we always saw cranes on that day.'

'Of course, of course, it wouldn't have been the same without the cranes! In the fields where the peas had been. The peas would already have been harvested, but plenty of them used to spill out of the ripe pods. So the cranes got them. Pa would wave his whip and' – spoken dreamily – 'off . . . they . . . would . . . fly . . .'

'You know what,' I said. 'I haven't seen any cranes for about twenty-five years. They simply aren't there. I'll be lying on my deathbed and suddenly remember that I never saw cranes again.'

'What are you on about? Deathbed, indeed!' commented Tonya with her usual bluntness. 'Just you stay alive!'

'I'm not thinking of dying, but if I haven't seen any cranes for the past twenty-five years, what guarantee is there that I'll see them in the next twenty-five? I can't even be sure that in twenty-five years time the three of us' – my sisters were over sixty then – 'will be peacefully playing cards together and reminiscing about Karavaevo.'

Each of us did some mental arithmetic and added twenty-five years to his or her age. In an instant things went very quiet around the table and throughout the whole house. At such moments people say that someone has just walked over their grave.

Tonya quickly rescued us from the situation: 'All right, all right. Let's deal. We'll play one hand and go to bed.'

But no one felt like dealing or playing any more.

Early the next morning I went out to my car which was in the road. I was going to look for mushrooms. I lifted the bonnet, filled the radiator and checked the oil.

At that moment a strange noise at the other end of the village attracted my attention. Surprisingly, before I had quite identified the noise, somehow I already knew what it was and that it could not be anything else. As I turned my head I knew exactly what I was going to see.

Nevertheless, I still could not believe my eyes. Unbelievable, dreamlike birds with long necks, huge birds (because they were so low) were flying over the very roofs of the houses from the other end of the village. They were not flying in any precise formation, simply in a broad flock like jackdaws or crows – but no, these were neither jackdaws nor crows.

The bell-tower divided the flock into two for a moment as they passed to left and right of it; but it was quickly behind them, after which they were heading straight for our house with its iron roof and brick chimney above the stove.

All at once the birds banked over on one wing and started flying in circles and curves, swirling like a whirlpool over our roof and chimney. With every circle they went higher and at the same time moved a little more to the south.

People began to fill the street. I remember my neighbour,

Alexander Nikolaevich, shouting: 'Cranes! Cranes! Nineteen of them!'

Another neighbour, Marusya Kuzova, for some reason began to count the number of times they circled: ten, twelve, fourteen. . . .

I was unable to count either the birds or the times they circled. I watched what was happening, unable to believe my eyes. My sisters came running out too. Katyusha had tears in her eyes, tears of excitement, I suppose, but also because she remembered the previous evening's conversation as she watched.

Then Tonya said in her abrupt way: 'There you are. So much for what you were saying. . . .'

But still, what really did happen?

7

IN KARAVAEVO THE CHURCH FESTIVAL WAS HELD ON ASSUMP-
tion Day, but in the little hamlet of Brod ('on Brod', as
they say in our parts) they celebrated the autumn festival
of Cosmas and Damian.[12] There, in that little village of
fifteen houses strung out along a knoll above the river
(except for the bath-houses, which had skipped down on
to a meadow right next to the river), there was neither a
fair nor were there outdoor festivities with masses of
people; quite simply, though, every house was full of
visitors and hospitality. Relations would gather for quiet
meals together around the table. The table tops would be
scrubbed clean and cold snacks, meat dishes and small
carafes placed on them, with a samovar at the head; and
it was not twenty versts to Brod, but one single, admittedly
crooked, little verst.

From the side-windows of our house you could see the
road through the village, a green sweep with just the
double track left by cart-wheels cutting through it and,
beyond that, the line of houses which stood in close
succession on the other side of the road. White willows
grew in front of the houses, their rounded crowns
resembling green clouds. Because of the houses and tree-
tops the view from our windows was restricted. The
willows and the roofs barred the way to the great open
spaces. Then, on top of that, there was our lilac (described
in greater detail elsewhere), which was right outside the
windows. From the low, ground-floor windows only its
brown branches were visible; but on the level of the upper

windows it was curly and feathery and stretched out its green leaves towards the windows, adding clusters of fluffy blooms in spring which completely blocked out the wide world.

From Grandfather's bedroom window, however, your gaze met a lucky gap between the willows and the roofs (the lilac did not reach that far), and you immediately saw all the way to the horizon, where behind a dark line of forest could be seen a church like a little white pointed thimble. In front of the dark line of the forest the earth would shine bright green with the winter crops or bright gold with corn, or it might take on the tarnished gold colour of stubble, with tiny wheatsheaves stacked crosswise upon it, or appear velvety black after ploughing. In that very field, forever visible through the gap between the willows and the roofs, far, far away (as if viewed through the wrong end of a pair of binoculars, not that I had any binoculars then), there stood a windmill. In the mornings I would try to guess whether the sails of the windmill would be turning as I ran up to the window, or whether its crossed arms would be stationary. As far as I was concerned, the windmill was about the size of a matchbox and so, when my father once took me up to it, I was frightened by the way its gigantic bulk grew and Father and I became smaller beside it. Finally, I had to throw my head back in order to see the whole structure. The windmill door, which from Grandfather's bedroom looked like a dot or a little hole similar to a beehive entrance or even smaller, turned into a huge door made of planks. Then suddenly the sail was released and it drifted away from me practically into the clouds. How could I possibly recognize my morning toy in that giant of logs and boards whose roof had turned bright yellow, the colour of egg-yolk, under a dense growth of lichen?

The hamlet of Brod was the next geographical point after Karavaevo (or, if you like, before Karavaevo), to which a direct line of communication extended from my childhood home. There would be a straight line to it, were

I to decide to draw a radial plan: our two-storey house would be at the centre of the universe, with excursions in various directions progressively taking over the earth. The village, orchard, kitchen garden, fallow area, river and nearby wood, as they say, do not count. We are concerned only with other centres of population. What could I put at the centre of the universe if not my childhood home? Otherwise, where else, in what other part of that blank sheet of the universe could I have put myself? That is exactly how the plan should be: your house and yourself in the middle of the sheet of paper, with symbolic lines radiating out in various directions from you and the house. One to Karavaevo, another to Brod (a short little line), and after that there could be any number of them: to Albania, Paris, London, Vietnam, Bulgaria, Warsaw, Budapest, Frankfurt-on-Main, Cologne and Munich, the Pamir, the Tien Shan, the Kara Sea, Nizhnekolymsk and Yayutsk, Kiev, Leningrad, Kishinev, Tbilisi, Erevan, Baku, Dushanbe, Ashkhabad, Samarkand and Bukhara, Tobolsk and Tyumen, Copenhagen and New York, San Francisco, Los Angeles, San Diego, Washington, Michigan, Marseille and Nice, Aix-en-Provence and Strasbourg, Grenoble, Bristol, Belgrade, Prague, Bratislava, Ljubljana, Kansas City, Iowa City, Chicago and Stockholm, Göteborg and Peking, Bordeaux and Dresden. . . .

It seems impossible that there was a time when on the virgin sheet of my life but two little lines went out from the centre, one of twenty versts, the other of one.

It is not, though, just a question of versts. Perhaps even now, if everything resumed its rightful place on earth – Karavaevo, Brod, the watermill and windmill, Father with the cart, Mother, my brothers and sisters, the house, Grandfather, indeed that whole way of life, including the fair on Assumption Day – if all around were Russia as she was before she was disembowelled, bled dry and mutilated, not forgetting the cranes amongst the peas, perhaps, for the right to travel in a cart through that Russia as far as Karavaevo I would trade in the whole accumulated cobweb

of symbolic lines with all its Colognes, Londons and
Parises, and leave myself with nothing more than the
pathway through the grass to the cattle track and then on
down the steep, green hillside to the fast-flowing, crystal-
clear river, across which in the alder-green shade has been
placed a yellow log, cut flat on top, with a smooth handrail
added to make a simple footbridge. The grown-ups go
straight across it, their heads facing forward, holding the
handrail with one hand, but I have to make my way across
sideways, so it is hard for me to move my feet one after
the other and I have to lift both my little arms up to hold
the handrail. As I do this my father holds me by the back
of the collar without letting me feel his hand and I have
the impression I am crossing the river by myself. At the
same time, though, I am not going to slip off the bridge.

Anyhow, the line to Brod would be straight only on the
plan. In reality it was a crooked dirt path leading out to
the cattle track, past the fallow land, down the steep hill,
past the fir and pine forest (which has juniper bushes
bursting out of it on to the green slope), across that same
wooden footbridge and on over a wide, even meadow to
the kitchen gardens of Brod, which are followed by the
houses themselves. You have to go through the whole
village, passing in front of the windows of the houses,
because Grigory Ivanovich and Pelageya Nikolaevna's
house is the last one, right at the other end of the village.
After that the green meadows begin again, the meadows
of a Russia still (let me repeat) unmutilated and unspoilt.

In Grigory Ivanovich and Pelageya Nikolaevna's house
they knew how to treat guests. Grigory Ivanovich would
strut around the table, making sure everything was as it
should be, his own right hand never without a glass. He
was shortish and thickset, a tough old man with a broad,
grey beard which he kept short, although, no matter how
short it might be, it always turned up at the end. He
constantly stroked it from underneath with the back of his
left hand, moving from his Adam's apple upwards.

At the same time as he stroked his beard Grigory

Ivanovich would give a shake of the head. Sometimes only the second half of this extremely characteristic movement was performed: the head and beard shook, but the hand played no part. If Grigory Ivanovich were describing how something had happened, he would shake his head and toss up his short, sturdy beard with particular expressiveness. He would wear a loose linen shirt and a plaited belt with a comb hanging from it on a string. The traditional grandfather, in fact, like those you see in pictures.

Pelageya Nikolaevna, with a spotted kerchief tied around her head and wearing a dark dress (brown, possibly), constantly says: 'Have some of this. . . . You're welcome to try this. . . . There's brawn, there's meat jelly and mutton. . . .'

After a minute or two it would start again: 'Have some of this. Go on, try these little mushrooms, salted orange milk caps, young hare. Go on, have some. . . .'

That young hare, deep red in colour and served finely chopped, the bright orange milk caps which still had their natural colour thanks to skilled salting, as well as the strange-looking carafes that crowded together at the end of the table – these are the things I remember best of all about those sit-down meals they would give us in Brod.

My eldest sister, Alexandra Alekseevna (or as we called her at home, Shurínka), was married into that household, which meant another capitalist in the family, the miller, Grigory Ivanovich Lámonov.[13] He and his son – our brother-in-law, Mikhail Grigoryevich – ran the business together.

It is known that windmills were once an obligatory part of the Russian landscape, especially towards the south, in the areas around Orlov, Kursk, Voronezh and Ryazan, not to mention the Don and the Ukraine. In our parts, admittedly, watermills were preferred because we were surrounded by a dense network of quiet, clear rivers. On the Koloksha alone between Yuryev-Polsky and Ustye, a distance of some seventy versts, there were twelve watermills. Twelve dams, twelve millponds – a real cascade, as they might say now. Yet what a beauty it was, the Koloksha! Its water was kept high by the dams and it was clear and full of fish; but now it is really shallow, sickly, overgrown and covered in slime.

Yet there were windmills too. Are there any records giving the overall figures for watermills and windmills in Russia? It would be interesting to know, because that would give us the number of peasant households that once owned those watermills and windmills, only to be smashed to pieces, as well as the number of peasant families that were subsequently dispersed far and wide or, more commonly, annihilated.

I have come to think that the house, yard, apiary and the whole of Grigory Ivanovich's homestead could serve as the ideal pattern for other peasant homesteads (one horse, one cow, two pigs and, I should imagine, coming up to twenty acres of land).

Their house had one storey and was small, but still it was not one of those simple peasant houses of ours which are all built to the same pattern. Nowadays I would call it a small cottage. Three windows looked out in one direction and three in the other (so you can imagine the size of the place), and of course there was a kitchen with a Russian stove. Some self-taught painter, however, had plastered the front room and decorated it with lilies and water-lilies. It was a kind of small drawing-room. Also, a narrow gallery like a corridor led round two of the outside walls of the house and there was another well-appointed main room across the passage from the kitchen. At this point I should mention the three details I remember better than anything. The first is the view from the front windows. You could not see the village houses from there, or any sheds, fences or horizontal railings, but instead you saw something like a framed picture – greenery stretching into the distance, a meadow with a river which bends on its way across, a steep green hillock at the far side of the meadow with a pine wood at the very top (the source of the orange milk caps which filled the plate on the table and which had kept not only their colour but even, I think, their little circles when they were salted).

Although this landscape was clean, neat, fresh and green, there was really nothing special about it – a meadow, a hillock and a pine forest – but for me it was something different. I was used to looking out of my own windows on to a village street where there were houses, wattle-fences around the kitchen gardens, white willows, a well and the road itself passing down the middle; and if I looked out of the front windows I saw the church and church fence some fifty paces from the house.

The second wonder was the lilies and water-lilies on the walls and ceiling of the main room in the house, the drawing-room.[14] This drawing-room with its decorations seemed to me like some sort of fairy-tale palace, it was so different from everything else that was to be seen or that I had actually seen in any other village house.

The third thing that astonished me at the time and stuck in my memory is the ochre paint. The outside of the house, the porch, the floors, the five steps leading from the lobby to the yard and the handrail next to them – everything was painted in clean, bright, thick, shiny ochre. Since then I have encountered ochre paint like that, with a polished look and so smooth and resilient it seemed like ivory, only in fine Russian icons.

All these things taken together – the top quality, hard-wearing paint, the lilies and water-lilies on the drawing-room walls and ceiling, the well-kept meadow and the hillock on the other side of the windows – produced a feeling of unreality, rather as if they were toys to be played with. 'We will play for a while now and after that we'll return to real life in the village.'

The yard was no less neat and clean than the house. It was of compressed earth and always swept spotless. Not a scrap of rubbish or piece of straw was to be seen there – not bad for a peasant yard! The harness would shine with its polished horse brasses, and in the cowshed, pigsty, sheep-pen and stable there would always be fresh yellow straw. Every item, the horse collar, pitchfork, broom, tarantass, shaft-bow, wicker basket, pail for wheel-grease, the horse's brush and comb, the axe and everything down to the last trifle would be in its own special place.

We also had a house and yard, but our family had ten children in it instead of a single grown-up son, and with us everything seemed somewhat disordered and run-down in comparison with that ideal, toy-town household. Perhaps ours was set up in the expectation that the family's activities would grow, perhaps part of them had already lapsed before I came along, but everything there seemed somehow too far-flung and scattered. Even the details were different. In our house we had room for a shelf on which God knows what had been gathering dust for years: little glass bottles, jars and other discarded things. Apart from that, we lived with a cupboard in the lobby containing a similar rubbish-heap of unnecessary stuff. There was even a store-room full of it. I shall not bother to mention the attic. I excavated whole layers of our family's past civilization up there. At Grigory Ivanovich's such a thing would have been imposs-ible and certainly was not to be found. Everything was in use, everything was in place. My mother, Stepanida Ivanovna, got by as best she could. She looked after the family and things to do with the household, kept the iron and earthenware pots going into the stove, saw to the animal feed, pigswill and food for us, after which came the kitchen garden, vegetable beds, the washing and rinsing, work in the fields, children's illnesses and the job of lifting the beetroot, cabbages and cucumbers. . . . When she was lying in her coffin I saw for the first time that the wedding-ring on her finger had worn right down until it was no thicker than thin foil, and not for nothing. I do not know how it held together. It is not surprising, even if she did have sufficient strength to do the main things (harnessed to our family and household like a horse to a cart), that Stepanida Ivanovna did not perhaps have enough left over when it came to seeing to some sort of exemplary order in the house, without a speck of dust or scrap of rubbish anywhere, just sparkling ochre paint.

And my father, Aleksey Alekseevich? He had his horse, his ploughing, his harrowing, he had the sheaves to carry and then the threshing (not forgetting his little factories); but, on top of all that, there was the problem of Aleksey Alekseevich's character. In his final years, no matter how much Stepanida Ivanovna badgered him, no matter how often she reminded him that the winter had arrived and the firewood had still not been put by, he always gave the same answer from behind the partition where he lay: 'All right, all right, we won't go without firewood.'

Of course I could have made a slight mistake and, as they say, got things out of balance. It is possible that I am remembering my house and yard as it was in the later period when everything really had left the rails, and not as it was in my early childhood when our homestead was no less organized and ordered than Grigory Ivanovich's.

Grigory Ivanovich had a very large horse with white legs, called Chayka. She was a bay with a blaze on her forehead. He would harness her in the yard and get into his sledge with the gates still shut, because otherwise, when the gates were opened wide by his son or Pelageya Nikolaevna, he might not manage to get into the sledge. Chayka would take off and there was no stopping her, all you could hear was the sound of the little bells dying away in the distance. Shaking his head and beard and occasionally patting the beard from below with the back of his left hand (whilst holding a glass in his right hand), Grigory Ivanovich would tell guests how Chayka was once stolen:

'Well . . . I went for the horse in the morning. She was chained up on the fallow ground. The chain was there but Chayka had gone. . . . There were marks . . . bootmarks . . . . The earth was damp, you could see everything, but then there's the road and the river, that would be the end of the trail. Looking for her in these parts would have been pointless. . . . But Chayka was not some sort of needle in a haystack, there was no other horse like her in the world ... no, there wasn't ... so I went off round the horse fairs, I did ... Yuryev-Polsky, Kuzmin Monastery, Suzdal, Vladimir, Gavrilov Posad – wherever there was a horse fair, I went. I visited all the fairs and markets, I didn't miss one, not one. ... Then suddenly I saw her. ... There she was, my Chayka, harnessed to a cart, as respectable as they come. Well, I slipped off to the militia, told them the story and claimed the horse. Off I went with the militiamen to the market. Chayka's master said he didn't know a thing and that she was his horse. There was no way I could prove anything. A militiaman took us both thirty paces away and asked the other man: 'What's the name of the horse?' 'Palma,' he answers. 'Call her over,' the militiaman tells him. So the man started: 'Palma! Palma!' but Palma doesn't move a muscle. 'Now, you.' I just shouted out: 'Chay ... ka. ...' Up went her head! She neighed loud enough to fill the whole market – overjoyed she was. She pulled out her tether and came straight over to me, dragging the cart behind her. Well, everything was clear. ... 'Off with the harness, master, they've come for her. ...'

I cannot imagine that it was with any deep sense of satisfaction or feeling of having done his duty by our dear Soviet authorities that Grigory Ivanovich later handed Chayka over to be placed in the communal barn belonging to the collective farm (actually it was a large shed which had been quickly turned into a communal barn). There, along with the other Brod horses, she soon became the shadow of her former self.

Grigory Ivanovich's windmill was not an ordinary mill for grinding flour, but an oil-mill. In our parts in those days they still sowed a great deal of flax; but the point is not that it was sown (it could be sown now), but that the peasants themselves decided what to do with it, right down to the last seed and stalk. It did not have to be handed over to anyone anywhere and they were not forced to sell it. The peasants had oil made, if they could, from the fine silky linseed; then it was called neither vegetable oil nor linseed oil, but simply 'fasting oil' – oil you could have during the fast, as opposed to Russian butter made from cream and boiled. That is what they would say: if you go to the market, buy some fasting oil.

I do not know the agreement Grigory Ivanovich had with the peasants concerning his oil-mill. He most likely took a part of the oil in return for making it, and that was what his enterprise consisted of (I should hate to use the little word 'business'). Probably, though, that is not exactly what happened. People knew that a pood[15] of seed made, say, fifteen pounds of oil and twenty-five pounds of linseed meal. A tenth went to the miller for his work. That being the case, you did not have to wait whilst he processed your particular seed. You brought two poods of seed and collected what was due to you; and if some old lady had scraped together a few tiny handfuls of seed, she would take her share away in a little bottle afterwards just the same.

You would eat potatoes with fasting oil (it immediately turned them bright yellow), pancakes, cabbage, mush-rooms, horse-radish, onion, thick pea soup – they were all eaten with fasting oil. Apart from that there was a tasty treat which all the children in our area enjoyed: a piece of fresh rye bread with fasting oil poured on it and sprinkled with salt. The salt was large grained and pleasantly crunchy to the teeth. Or you could pour some oil into a saucer, sprinkle on the salt and dip the bread in it. . . .

I must admit I have forgotten the taste of fasting oil now and, no matter how hard I try, I cannot buy (or otherwise acquire) even one bottle anywhere. In the whole of the former state of Russia, now the USSR, you cannot buy a single mouthful of fasting oil! In the bottle the oil looked as black as tar with just the bright little golden bubbles of foam at the top to give away its true colour, a colour that fully revealed itself only when you poured a thin layer of it into a white saucer.

The stream of golden oil flowed in Grigory Ivanovich's mill for many years and so it is not surprising that this golden stream, as it was poured into innumerable buckets and quarters,[16] managed to produce a crystal-like precipitate of hard little discs, this time of genuine gold. When you talk to people about it, some say that Grigory Ivanovich collected together a heap of thirty such little discs, others say fifty. It could be that he perished because of them, although we always thought that they came for him because of a joke and we even knew which one. He was greasing the wheels of his cart when his brother, who lived two houses away and with whom they had previously had some sort of quarrel, came up to him and started complaining: 'That grease, Grigory, is not what it used to be. I used to grease the wheels once a week. Now I don't get as far as the forest before the wheels start creaking. What on earth is going on?'

Grigory Ivanovich gave a shake of his short beard and smoothed it from underneath with the back of his left hand: 'The grease is as good as the government.'

That was in the early 1930s – that is, after the collectivization and the liquidation of the kulaks, which the oil-miller survived unscathed, except of course that he had to part with his mill. They took the mill away from its owner but, just the same, after that it did not produce a single tumblerful of fasting oil. Instead it became more and more dilapidated and broken and finally disappeared from the face of the earth.

The version of events which says that they came unexpectedly for Grigory Ivanovich and did not give him a minute alone with Pelageya Nikolaevna – and that he did not therefore have the opportunity to whisper to her where his little golden discs were buried in the yard – that version of events is untrue. By that time everyone was so obedient and subdued that the people carrying out the arrest did not have to go to Brod. All they had to do was send a summons: come to such and such a place. When this happened the man would go on his own voluntarily, even though he knew he would not be coming back. So Grigory Ivanovich would have had the time to tell Pelageya Nikolaevna the secret of his buried treasure; and if he did not tell her, it means that he was afraid that they would frighten his old lady and she would give the secret away, or in his heart of hearts he hoped that they would release him after all.

At that time an intense, criminal hunt was on for those little golden discs throughout the villages of Russia. You might have two of them or even five, just the same the state in its pettiness could not rest until those little discs were in its hands. In the villages around Ryazan, Orlov, Tambov and Vladimir and in every other village they arrested people, frightened and tormented them until they admitted where their crock of gold was hidden. Sometimes they let people go after they had told them; but of course Grigory Ivanovich admitted nothing, that is not the sort of man he was.

Pelageya Nikolaevna lived on for a few more years after Grigory Ivanovich received his summons and went away never to return. She was left on her own, as their only heir, Mikhail Grigoryevich, went off to live in a small mining town somewhere. One can understand well enough why he did that: it cannot be easy to watch the gradual impoverishment and destruction of your family home, livelihood and all the places you knew as a child. The house, left without its real master, was sold and resold, to be finally inhabited by a local fool called Holy Vasya, a total nonentity. In the old days Grigory Ivanovich would not have allowed Holy Vasya even as far as the porch. If Grigory Ivanovich were to come back to life and find out that Holy Vasya lived in his house now, I should think he would immediately die all over again.

Nowadays, in place of a sturdy nest inhabited by peasant folk, there is just a pile of rotten wood which still just about resembles a house from the outside. Apart from that, it is surrounded by nettles. Any orchards or apiaries are out of the question; but since the entire village of Brod is gradually wasting away anyway, the rotting pile of wood and the nettles do not produce a particularly depressing effect. Today the whole of Brod is full of piles of rotten wood and nettles.

On the contrary, a sturdy and beautiful peasant house would look wrong and stand out now. It would not fit in with the nettles and holes which have taken the place of the houses. As things are today, though, there is complete harmony and unity of tone: nettles and holes instead of houses, abandoned orchards running wild. Soon they will flatten and plough up the very place where the village of Brod once stood, just as they are ploughing under hundreds, even thousands, of similar little hamlets. Some representative of a later generation will look at the flat fields, unaware that this spot had once been full of life and song and busy festivals, unaware that windows with beautiful decorative casings used to be here, that there were cocks crowing, apple and cherry trees in blossom, carts creaking and windmills turning. He will look upon the flat, ploughed land exactly as we look upon the regular waves of the sea which cover the spot where, theoretically, there once flourished the fabled land of Atlantis.

8

I WAS LUCKY AS FAR AS MY EARLIEST RECOLLECTIONS OF life on earth are concerned. Had I popped up somewhere in the vicinity of smoky factory chimneys on the outskirts of a town, where the trains clanged, the ground was thick with oil and the leaves of the trees, like the little huts above the cesspits, were covered with soot, then. . . . Then, too, childhood would have been childhood and it would have had its little specks of gold, even despite the alehouses full of drunks that you find on the outskirts of a town, despite the hungry stray dogs, bad language and family quarrels, the fights and the crime. . . . But I was met on earth by quiet and peaceful creativity.

If you plant a tiny seed in the ground and grow something from it – an ear of rye, a panicle of oats, a branching stem of flax with its little blue flowers, even a fat, dumpy beetroot – that in itself is wonderful; but, apart from that, it means constant sensitivity to the weather and a constant feeling of closeness to the land and nature. You wait for the rain and are overjoyed when it finally comes; you wait for fine weather and its arrival brings more joy; melting snow, frosts, the movement of storm-clouds, the subtle colours of sunset, the behaviour of animals and grasses, spiders and frogs, darkening sandstone and smoke as it emerges from a chimney; then there is the dew on the grass and the bubbles in puddles when it rains. . . . All of that is necessary not simply for you to enjoy nature or observe it in a detached sort of way, even if you were a student of phenology or Prishvin[17] himself, no, it is work, everyday existence, life itself.

I read this in a contemporary magazine:

If a person spends a long time in a car or aeroplane, he becomes drowsy, listless and loses his appetite and ability to work. Why does this happen? Results obtained from experiments conducted with animals and people enable us to conclude that the size of the surrounding electric field has a great effect on people's mood and the way they feel. In the interiors of cars and aeroplanes the strength of the electric field is significantly less than in the world outside, since those areas are screened off by a metallic casing.

Researchers tried artificially increasing the strength of the electric field in a metallic cage containing experimental animals. A special generator produced inside the cage an electric field of 500-800 v/m, the normal intensity of the earth's own electric field. Following this, the level of activity and vitality of the experimental animals increased significantly. Analogous results were obtained when such experiments were conducted using people.

Conducting experiments with people is on the whole considered immoral; but what can you do if the people voluntarily put themselves into various metallic cages and cut themselves off from the earth and its integrated electric and other forces?

Nowadays we have eccentrics who go to bed with bare wires linking their ankles to the radiators of the central-heating system. Somewhere down below in one way or another the radiators are in contact with the earth via pipes; and so a person living, say, on the eighth floor is able to earth himself artificially and thus satisfy an urge to be joined to the earth, to touch it, if not by walking barefoot on a path across a field or by immersing his whole body in the sweet-scented grass of a meadow, then at least by availing himself of wires and heating pipes.

By means of synthetic clothing and footwear, rubber

73

tyres, asphalt and all manner of plastics man is isolating himself more and more from the earth, cutting himself off artificially not only from its overall electric field but from a great many other uninvestigated forces which are produced by the trees and the grass, by rain and rainbows, pine needles and passing clouds, slumbering evergreen forests and morning dew, mist on the river, lightning . . . yes, and simply by the good soft soil.

Yet this physical isolation seems trivial when you think of the monstrous mutual isolation that exists between Man and the Earth on the psychological and spiritual plane. Of course we try, we make some sort of effort and grow a flower on the balcony or an onion to add a bit of greenery, we may even have a plant in the apartment or acquire a bit of land with a dacha and on Sundays we get out to a wood or the river; but none of that amounts to a serious relationship with the earth. It is all like a children's game of mothers and fathers instead of genuine love, genuine caresses and genuine childbirth.

It is amazing to think that my grandfather and even my father enjoyed that direct and immediate contact with the earth which man is supposed to have and needs to have. . . . We simply cannot remember how much land our family had. I ask my elder brothers and sisters and they give me different answers, but the general picture is somewhere between fifteen and thirty acres. That was the microscopic piece of land which was, so to speak, entrusted to our family. We had to see that it prospered, turn it, plant it with seeds, remove the weeds, manure it, look after its every need and caress it.

This would be the time to write about the various forms of peasant labour I occasionally experienced but the trouble is I have already said practically everything there is to say about them in my previous books, look at *A Drop of Dew* alone. I admit that the reader of these lines may not have come across a book with such a title and that therefore there would be no repetition as far as he was concerned, but I know myself of the existence of that 'lyrical tale', with its detailed impressions of childhood in a peasant family in the country, and my pen would immediately refuse to move across the paper as soon as it felt itself on a familiar path.

My general feeling as I unfold the material from which I intend to fashion this book, spreading it out on a large imaginary table, is one of horror that it should be so full of gaping holes. I have been cutting out piece after piece from the long canvas of my life without any order, just as the whim took me, and sewing a story, a poem, a chapter of a book or an episode in a novel from them. It was as if I were taking a birch, a river, a camomile flower, a lark, a well, or the little bell-tower beyond the dark-blue forest and presenting these separate details of landscape in the hope that a complete picture would gradually assemble. Well, there was sense in that, if only I did not now have the idea of depicting the entire composition of the landscape from start to finish, so the question now is what to do with the birch tree, river, camomile, lark, well and bell-tower beyond the dark-blue forest, all of which have already been described?

Of course, in the space of twenty-four hours (not to mention a year and even less a whole lifetime), the lighting changes and by evening objects may look differently from the way they did at midday or in the morning, and in the autumn when the leaves fall things do not look as they did in July but, nevertheless, that is cold comfort and would hardly justify my going ahead and writing about everything a second time. However, as I summon up my earliest impressions, those I received before the age of seven and before the turning-point (actually there were two simultaneous turning-points – school and collectivization), I have to admit that there is little I remember of the peasants' work in the fields, provided I am conscientious and refuse to drag any of my later experience into that early part of my life. My chief impressions were evidently gained at that time from the house and the domestic routine; and of first importance here were not the details or factual information, but the sense of well-being, of warmth, light, family, happiness, God. . . .

The two-storey house (the lower part was brick, the upper wood), built around the middle of the last century, turned to dust as its centenary approached. At any rate all the wood in it turned to dust. Apart from that, the iron roof rusted through, its ties disintegrated, the wind forced up the iron sheets and made them clatter, and when it rained basins and wash-tubs had to be placed throughout the house. At this point I might strike a plaintive note: the earth has few sounds that could be as sweet to my ear as the noise made by the rain on the iron roof of my house; but I discovered that it is only sweet when things are cosy, warm and dry beneath the roof, for the pleasure turned into a sense of calamity and anguish of soul. It was worth restoring stability and strength to my parents' house – as indeed my soul desired – simply in order to hear, if only once again, with a peaceful mind and heart, the sound produced by the rain on the roof of my home, whether it were a summer storm with its large drops or, indeed, just a soft, steady drizzle.

By 1961 (I already had five or six books behind me and two daughters of pre-school age) the problem had become totally clear: I had either to abandon altogether the home that had nurtured me, take on some dacha or other near Moscow and never again return to Alepino, or repair the house and go there every summer. Our river was there, along with our hills and ravines, our woods on the hills, our white willows and limes, flowers and pathways. . . . And of course there was our village cemetery where Aleksey Alekseevich had already been at rest for four years by that time and where Stepanida Ivanovna was to be laid to rest, as it later turned out, in another five years. I decided to repair the house in Alepino.

This was not a practical step but a romantic one. Everyone said that it would be cheaper and easier to build a house in a different place, even if still in Alepino. It would be more straightforward and I would have a new, compact house, designed for convenience. It would be senseless and stupid to stick to the outsize dimensions of Grandfather's house and attempt to modernize it. Nothing would come of it. Nevertheless, I opted to keep to Grandfather's dimensions.

Did I give any thought to the fact that it would just the same be a different house, even if it did retain its exterior aspect? Perhaps I did realize this, but I still failed to foresee that momentary feeling of alarm I had the instant I opened the door and stopped on the threshold of our newly restored 'bottom half' (the lower quarters, the ground floor), where a new floor had already been laid and the ceiling and brick walls replastered. I stopped on the threshold and realized that everything which belonged there was to go into an empty three-dimensional space: length, breadth and height. The lowish oblong box was absolutely empty. The four small windows with their new frames and sills did not disturb the sense of something just created and sterile where what had been *no longer* was and what was to be had *not yet* appeared. A new start could be made.

Could it really be that the myriad different impressions which made up the intricate world of my childhood, could it be that the world which had been contained in that house with its nooks and crannies, partitions and beds, benches, shelves, stoves, cupboards, cast-iron pots, oven prongs, logs, paraffin lamps, with its harness (smelling of tar), samovars, chests, hot flapjacks in the mornings, icons at night lit by little ever-burning lights, cloth coats, sheepskin coats, boots, small ovens (full of dried-out mittens, foot bindings and socks), cockroaches behind the ovens, sieves, choppers (to chop splinters), felt boots with reinforced soles, windows iced up like icebergs, with my brothers and sisters, with kittens, lambs and calves (we would take a calf into the house during the winter and keep it there for the first two or three weeks of its life), with its oblong washing-tubs, its brooms, its leavened dough and hot bread, its clouds of white steam every time the door was opened, with its interior frames for the windows which were removed in the spring just before Easter, could it really be that all this had fitted into something the size of that miserable empty box: length, breadth, height?

And what shape would the soul be if one undertook a similar repair job on it and threw out all that had been accumulated and lived with so as to leave it, if only for a while, just as empty and open to view? Could the soul really turn out to be three-dimensional, like that strange and frightening parallelepiped? Would it all come down to mere geometry and my thousands on thousands of impressions of the external world not go beyond the boundaries of length, breadth and height?

Do not agree with it, my soul, protest!

The house had two storeys. It had an upstairs and a downstairs: that was how we called them – not the first floor and not the lower or ground floor, but the upstairs and the downstairs. . . . 'Go upstairs', Stepanida Ivanovna might say to one of her daughters, 'and water the flowers.' 'Where have the scissors disappeared to?' 'They're downstairs on the window-sill.' A narrow staircase led from the downstairs to the upstairs, it had one bend and fourteen steps in all. Down below, it began at a thin narrow door with a revolving catch (to prevent its opening by itself), and at the top . . . at the top it ended with nothing in particular, you simply stepped up from the highest step on to the floor and that was the upstairs.

The downstairs was a continuation of the yard and lobby (and beyond the yard was the orchard-cum-kitchen garden, and beyond that the fields, the earth), but the upstairs was the beginning of something different, totally different, something unconnected with the earthly, kitchen-garden world. It contained a beautiful china cupboard, or more accurately sideboard, a sofa, a spacious table (adjustable in length, by the way), a long cover on the chest of drawers embroidered with red butterflies, table-cloths, also embroidered (for feast-days), broad-wicked 'lightning' paraffin lamps, a mirror with a small table beneath it full of beautiful knick-knacks, a special step-shaped stand for potted plants, books by Pushkin and Lermontov, a Bible that Grandfather would constantly read in his room, using a large magnifying glass with a handle, a walnut wardrobe and walnut bed in the so-called 'middle room' (on which bed, incidentally, I was born on the Day of the Holy Spirit) and bookcases in the 'back' room belonging to the girls.

This was the scheme of things. The earth is the earth. Fields, orchard, kitchen garden. From out of the earth grew the tree of our house, of our family, of our kin. It sank its roots down into the earth: the yard with its little huts for a cow, horse and sheep, with its carts and harness, sties and straw, manure and hay, pitchfork and harrow, plough and axe. . . .

Apart from all that, Grandfather, Aleksey Dmitrievich, fixed up half of a small discarded oblong tub under the roof of the yard so that pigeons would live there. That was done for the soul and should be looked upon as not strictly necessary. Still, the pigeons came to live there; they would coo, peck at the oats spilt on the swept cobble-stones of the yard (the centre of the yard was paved with stones from the river), fly out of the semi-darkness of the yard through the open gates into the blindingly bright summer daylight and afterwards return from the blue sky – from, in order of flowering, the lilac and the white willows, the bird-cherry, then the limes – back into the safe gloom of the yard. Our Alepino house, repaired now for lightning summer visits, no longer has any yard at all, but above an upper window behind the decorative casing there live an obstinate pair of pigeons. Could they be the descendants of Grandfather's? Could they, along with their genes, have inherited visions, visions of an old man with a grey beard and a broom, of a black stallion, a harness, of spilt oats and of a fair-haired little lad making his way barefoot over the cold, damp stones to the back gate which stands open to the sunny, green and warm orchard?

So, the tree of the house sank the roots of the yard into the earth and in this way stood firmly on the ground. The lobby, as a continuation of the yard (with its store-rooms, flour bins, sacks, buckets, tubs and household equipment in general), and then the downstairs part of the house (as a continuation of the yard and lobby), where there was a Russian stove as well as armfuls of wood, full and half-length sheepskin coats on pegs, earthenware containers for washing, huge cast-iron pots of mash for the cows, the cooking and the samovar which produced pungent bluish fumes, wide benches and equally wide shelves, sieves and a kneading-trough, peelings and other food waste, a broom standing at the threshold, myriads of flies on summer days, earthenware jars of milk and pots of soured cream, brawn (for which boiled meat would be boned before feast-days), steamed cabbage and turnips, thick pea soup and buckwheat porridge, potato soup and rough-and-ready everyday pies (carrot, potato, turnip), kitchen towels and washing-up, a big wooden trough for washing clothes (which had been washed so much they almost had holes in them) and a wash-stand, this downstairs part of the house together with the lobby I would describe as the trunk of the tree which was fixed to the earth by the roots of the yard. But after that came the first floor, the 'upstairs'. Here were the leaves, blossom and fruit. Yes, it was a completely different world, both to look at and, more importantly, in essence. The roots were in the ground, but the blossom was open to the sun and wind and was the result of all the tree's efforts – of the roots, the trunk and the surrounding world combined. And then, after the blossom, come the apples. Of course what the apples are like depends on the particular sort of tree it is, but it has to be said that by the time of Russia's destruction (when all her roots were chopped through, her branches lopped short and her trunk hacked to pieces), the upper layer of the peasantry had started actively and, I should say, productively sending shoots up into the superstratum of the Russian intelligentsia and Russian culture. Esenin, Klyuev, Chaliapin, Korin and

Sokolov-Mikitov are not the only examples. The heroine of Mayakovsky's poem ('I'll come at four,' said Maria, 'eight, nine, ten'), that same Maria, a member of the intelligentsia and a beauty, was the daughter of a Voronezh peasant.[18] Well, Solzhenitsyn's parents were in reality peasants (although by then they belonged to the intelligentsia too); he was born in 1918, yet it is in no way thanks to Soviet power, but rather in spite of it, that he became what he is. Of course as a Russian cultural and historical phenomenon it would have been distinct in character, but there can be no doubt that it would have been a phenomenon. The genes of the upper stratum of the peasantry (I repeat) had started to move, to become active and send forth shoots into the cultured layer of the people. Now one can make only guesses and suppositions as to the possible outcome of this process. As is known, the whole of that upper stratum of the peasantry – fifteen million people in number – was deliberately cut off in 1929, cut off and thrown to torment and death in the deserted lands of the tundra. Even so, take any of the more talented people of our time and, as they say, scratch the surface, and you will realize immediately that he and all the rest should be looked upon as chance survivors: Boris Kornilov, Pavel Vasilyev, Andrey Platonov, Tvardovsky, Fatyanov, Lukonin, Abramov, Astafyev, Alekseev, Rasputin, Belov, Yashin . . . your obedient servant. . . . If one were to do some serious statistical research, one could collect scores of names, not only in literature but in related arts and in science (especially), but of course these would be the names of those who survived by chance and not of those who were deliberately and maliciously destroyed. Their names we shall never discover.

And so this is the upper storey of the house – the crown, leaves, blossom and apples, the result of many years, or rather many centuries of effort by the tree. Here there is no steam, nor are there fumes or the clatter of dishes, or the gurgle of water, or left-overs, or rubbish, or clouds of frosty air from the street every time the door is opened, or outdoor shoes at the threshold, or sheepskins on the peg, or buckets of water, or a calf behind the stove. . . . Here the walls are painted with gloss paint (royal blue), there is a snow-white plaster ceiling with a patterned cornice, flowers and beautiful furniture, a tiled stove, gilded icons in the farthest corner and bright homespun mats on the floor. There is cleanliness, quiet and, most important of all, leisure: leisure and a festive feeling.

There were no spongers or loafers in our large family. Even Grandfather Aleksey Dmitrievich, whose age would suggest he ought to get along simply watching others work or, if he were going to help them, then only with advice or general organization, even he, from the moment he got up – that is, from dawn – would be on his feet in the yard, either with a broom in his hands or with a pitchfork (making a mixture of straw and hay), or he would be there at the woodpile, or chopping brushwood on the block, or drawing water from the well. . . . There was enough work for all of Aleksey Alekseevich's sons and daughters (whilst still only teenagers the girls would use the harrow, make and rake hay, weed beds, pull flax, tidy up at home, stand on the cart as the hay was being gathered in or, if we were transporting sheaves of wheat, hand them up to Father on the wagon). . . . I might have been only four or five years old but I still had my share of work, even if it simply amounted to myself and my elder brother holding up a sack (really I was holding on to the sack) whilst my father repeatedly thrust a double-ended wooden scoop, shiny with age, into a golden heap of grain, took some of it up and threw it from the scoop into the sack in such a way that every time he threw some it felt rather like a punch against my small hands which were not yet strong, although they managed to keep a tight grip.

Our peasant smallholding was not, however, as gluttonous and greedy a machine as all that. There was leisure occasionally and free time turned up even during summer, not to mention the long winter evenings. One of my elder sisters (everyone in my family is older than I, I was an afterthought, a final attempt) had been a grammar-school girl in the provincial capital of Vladimir (they abolished the province of Vladimir and created the IIR – the vast Ivanovo Industrial Region), another – in the year I was born, as it happens – had fallen off a horse and hurt her spine badly. She lay some time in plaster and even for a few years after that could not bend over, run, walk quickly or, especially, work. She was surrounded by books: Pushkin and Lermontov (in fine single-volume editions with illustrations), Aleksey Konstantinovich Tolstoy,[19] Polonsky, Apukhtin. . . . Life is going on down below as usual, whilst upstairs where we are everything is peace and quiet. Grandfather is moving his enormous magnifying glass to and fro across the pages of the Bible and I am with Katyusha out of his way in the other room: although it would be truer to say that Katyusha is with the books whilst I go round and about her like a kind of kitten. She would read poetry out loud all the time – whether for herself or with an eye to the fair-haired three-year-old who was there with her I cannot say – but they had a shock when suddenly, before I could read and before I knew even a single letter, I began to recite by heart whole pages from 'The Demon', as well as 'Tamara', 'An Angel Flew across the Midnight Sky', 'The Water-Nymph' and 'The Sail'. It could well be that I did not understand the meaning of the verse I had learnt by heart from Katyusha's lips and simply recited it (whilst not articulating every word), but I remember a sky covered in ragged black thunder-clouds, in the middle of which was a huge, extremely bright moon.

I said 'leisure and a festive feeling'. And, indeed, our upstairs came to life on feast-days. The yellow varnished table was moved apart or, more accurately, opened up and covered with a white table-cloth. People set about carting up plates and dishes from down below (where the stove had been burning from the previous evening whilst food of all kinds was being prepared, starting with brawn, fish in jelly, leg of mutton cooked in pastry, shredded cabbage, and ending with home-made biscuits, pies and buns). Wineglasses and decanters were placed round the white table-cloth. The liqueurs were Father's own and made from lemon peel, cherries, rowan-tree berries and St John's wort. A keg of home-brewed mead (*kumushka*) would already have gurgled its fill as it fermented for three days on the stove and by now would have been made good and cold in the lobby. If, say, we take the Feast of the Protection, which was our church festival, the weather would already be so cold that there would be no need to put the keg in water in order to cool it, as there would be on any of the summer feast-days.

The bells would finish ringing for the early morning service (the bell-tower was fifty paces or less from our house), and after that they would ring for the Liturgy and again stop. A member of the household would keep an eye on the window: the Liturgy would be a long time ending. But then the first men and women church-goers would appear on the front porch of the church. They would take their time as they went off along the various paths towards their small, cosy villages amid our picturesque, equally cosy hills. Many of them, however, would go to houses in our village – not only the houses' inhabitants, but guests too. A small string of guests would also make their way towards our house. The Buryakovs from Shunovo were relatives, so were the Lámanovs[20] from Brod, relatives mostly through marriage. Aleksey Alekseevich's daughter married and went there, as did his sister. . . . For the same reason Alexander Sergeevich Smirnov was always a possible guest in our house, as he too had married into the Soloukhin family; but I must speak separately about him and the imaginary line that stretched across the countryside from our house to Peksha (now the town of Kolchugino).

I do not know why and how it happened, but way back in Grandfather Aleksey Dmitrievich's time the Soloukhin family began to establish links with classes other than the peasantry. For example, Grandfather's sister, Darya

Dmitrievna, married the rich merchant Kurov (a real merchant's name) and went to live in Nizhny Novgorod, and Grandfather's daughter (in other words, my father's sister), Vera Alekseevna, went so far as to become a noblewoman when Alexander Sergeevich Smirnov, a landowner from Petrishchevo, asked for her hand. Their estate was in Petrishchevo, but by the time I was a child there was, naturally, no question of any estate. They lived in the small industrial town of Peksha (which, let me repeat, is now the town of Kolchugino), in their own little wooden house with a small garden and vegetable patch. They had two delightful little girls called Vavulka and Lika (Valentina and Lidia), who of course were my cousins. Lika was born the same year as I and Vavulka was two years older.

There was only the one link between our village dwelling and the small house in Peksha but it took on different appearances. Uncle Sasha would come to us from Peksha on foot, a walk of twenty-five kilometres over land which was still beautiful and unsullied, which was not yet covered with rubbish, nettles, tangled weeds and junk, which had not yet been pitted with holes or left stinking of solar oil, or spoilt by tractors and heavy vehicles (like the village streets are now, in particular), or poisoned with various herbicides and pesticides. The small villages on the way were still intact, undecayed and well looked after. The bell-towers and churches were also in one piece and looked like toys where they stood on the hills and the evening bells still rang out over the land as it fell silent at the approach of sunset. It even occurs to me that the twenty-five kilometre walk might have been Uncle Sasha's main motive. On top of that, he was very fond of bathing in our local river, which was still crystal clear, in the pool we called 'The Wash-tub'. To this day I can see his contented, even blissful face with its moustache and spectacles above the smooth black surface of the calm water. Then of course one or two glasses of our home-made liqueur (after a walk like that and the swim) no doubt also had a certain appeal for Uncle Sasha. In short, he really enjoyed visiting our village, but he always came on foot and always in the heat of summer. The age of tarantasses, summer droshkies and other types of carriage had been left behind before I arrived on the scene.

My father, on the other hand, would harness up our Golubchik to the sledge or the cart (according to the season) for his visits to Peksha, which would be in the autumn or winter months (and he would always take me with him). Father and I would slowly wend our way over those twenty-five kilometres, spending virtually a whole day at it, and the end of the journey was always the same. Father would say: 'Look now, I am letting go of the reins. Golubchik will find the route himself.'

And that was exactly what happened. Without getting lost in the streets of the town (which had single-storey buildings, by the way), taking all the correct turnings, Golubchik would bring us to Uncle Sasha and Aunt Vera's house, a house also inhabited by two delightful little girls, Vavulka and Lika, my cousins.

Uncle Sasha, a typical representative of the Russian intelligentsia, was a most gentle-mannered, kind, warm-hearted man with an equally gentle sense of humour. Seeing his small daughter at her homework, he would say, for example: 'Vavulka, surely you are not doing homework, are you?'

'Yes, Papa, I am doing my homework.'

'Well, just stop it. Better go for a walk. Do you really still go to school?'

'Of course I do.'

'Well, stop that too! It must be so boring for you. Surely it's much more interesting to play with the other little girls.'

'Papa! What if our teacher heard what you are saying . . .'

'Of course your teacher is too old to run about with the girls, so she makes you all sit at your lessons. But don't you do it!'

I imagine he spoke like that only with Vavulka, a diligent worker. Such a conversation would have been impossible with Lika, who as it was could not wait to abandon her homework and run out into the street to play with the other girls.

What was there for a member of the Russian intelligentsia to do if he had not been finished off in the early years of Soviet power and had not emigrated? He could become an accountant. So Uncle Sasha worked in the accounts office of some loathsome local branch of the timber industry, until the person working opposite him in the poky accountants' room informed on him because of some joke. That was the end of Uncle Sasha, of Alexander Sergeevich Smirnov.

Yet during my early childhood years he was still alive and joking and on warm summer days would unexpectedly appear at our house in Alepino and swim in the river, grunting with bliss, his black moustache raised above the water along with his spectacles, also black, which he wore because he was short-sighted.

I started to talk about Uncle Sasha in connection with the guests we would have in our house in Alepino at the time of a church festival – say, at the Feast of the Protection; but it occurs to me now that, really, Uncle Sasha was most likely not there. For some reason, I do not recall his ever sitting amongst a mass of guests at a crowded table. I always remember him alone, making his way, as if he were out for a stroll, first along the path from Negodeikha, then over the meadow on the other side of the river, and after that up the hill from the river to the village. . . . Well, if the newly established regime feared, hated and exterminated people like that in order to protect itself. . . . There was, though, some sort of logic in it. This newly established anti-national and anti-Russian regime needed of course to destroy as many of the best and finest people it possibly could.

On the most important festivals the upstairs table would be laid for guests. It was at that table, then, that a funny little thing happened to me which for some reason I seem to recall as happening to someone else. They probably told me about it on a number of occasions when I was still quite small and the image has remained in my memory as if I had been a witness to the event rather than its central character.

It seems it took a long time to wean me from my mother's breast. Let us say this happened on the Feast of the Protection – well then, I was already sixteen months old. And so, whilst the holiday banquet was in progress, my mother picked me up and I began to demand what I wanted, working away at her with my little hands. At this point someone made a joke. (Now that could have been Uncle Sasha, in fact, or Mikhail Grigoryevich Lamanov, our brother-in-law from Brod, who also liked to joke): 'He should be ashamed of himself, a grown-up fellow like that and still after the breast. It's time for him to drink *kumushka*. Come on, give him some *kumushka* instead of milk. . . .'

My mother took a teaspoonful of *kumushka* and, at the very moment I was about to get what I craved, poured it into my mouth. They say I coughed and cried but after that I never once demanded the breast or took it. Sometimes I even joke to myself that in my case the transition to alcohol took place immediately after I finished with breast milk.

At the end of such occasions the noise of the banquet would draw to a close. . . . In what way, though? Well, naturally, they would talk, quietly and with dignity, perhaps they might even sing songs, but real songs, without the racket we have these days (as when they sing 'Oh, How They Sang and Played at the Wedding!'). In those days, of course, many people knew how to sing properly because the Church gave them a real training in music; you were not allowed to caterwaul in church but had actually to sing there. My mother, Stepanida Ivanovna, had a particularly good voice. 'The Cold Waves Lap', 'Now the Morning Has Broken, the Waters Turn Red',

'Why Has the Bright Dawn Grown Dim?', 'In the Little Low Room', 'The Little Grey Dove Moans', 'Not the Fine Autumn Rain', 'Do Not Sew for Me, Mother' – these are the songs that were sung in our house. So the noise and hum of the banquet would die away, all the dirty dishes would be carried downstairs and a blessed calm would once again return upstairs. Grandfather would get down to the Bible with his huge magnifying glass on a handle and Katyusha and I would pore over our books.

It would be unfair of me to maintain that there was nothing downstairs apart from pots, mash for the cows, bundles of firewood and the kneading-trough, and that the poetry was exclusively upstairs.

Lying on the stove next to my mother (during her rare moments of leisure) I heard more poetry, but Katyusha and Mother were keen on different things. In a rather hurried, spluttering voice, garbling some of the words and even some lines, my mother would recite to me (by heart, unlike Katyusha, who had the benefit of beautiful books) all about Uncle Vlas who wandered throughout Russia, collecting money for God's churches so that his sins would be forgiven, about the unreaped strip of rye and about how:

> The evening fell, the stars were shining,
> All around the frost bit hard,
> Through the village came an infant,
> Blue and trembling with the cold.
>
> In that village an old woman
> Saw the orphan in the street,
> Gave him shelter at her fireside,
> Gave him also food to eat.

On that warm stove, when the frost outside really was biting hard, things were just right for my infant soul to receive its first lessons in compassion and kindness. . . .

Upstairs, where the flowers, the 'lightning' lamp and the mirror with the table beneath were to be found, it would be: 'Who is galloping hard through the cold and the gloom?/A horseman out late and a young boy, his son'; upstairs: 'Where the willows bend low o'er the river, /Where the sun in the summer beats down,/The dragonflies flutter and quiver,/As gaily they circle around. . . ./Come, child, come to us, come on over,/For we want to teach you to fly,/Come, child, come to us, do not waver,/For your mother a-sleeping does lie.' Upstairs: 'I love a storm in early May,/The first spring thunder in the air'; upstairs: 'Misty morning, hoary morning'. . . . Downstairs, where beneath one were the warm bricks of the stove and the cockroaches waggled their whiskers in the dark corners, it was: 'See, here is my village,/In this house I dwell,/And now in my toboggan I am sliding down the hill', 'What, asleep, countryman? Now that spring has arrived and your neighbours/Have long been at work?' Downstairs: 'You sang all the time, and that was fine,/Now let us see how you dance'; downstairs: 'People through the streets are going,/Hard-earned pennies in their hand,/From those pennies, quickly growing,/Spring God's temples o'er the land'.

The poems were different but they were created by one people, just as there was one house and one roof and I, too, was one whole, unique person.

9

'WHERE DO YOU THINK GOD IS, THEN? JUST IN HEAVEN? Well, actually, he is everywhere.' This is what my mother, Stepanida Ivanovna, would impress upon me. 'He'll pretend to be a beggar – say, Mishka from Zelnikovo, and he'll ask alms of you and you'll give him a piece of bread. You'll think you gave the bread to Mishka from Zelnikovo, but it was Jesus Christ all the time. At Judgement Day he'll recognize you and give you a smile. "I know that boy," he'll say. "When I was hungry he gave me a piece of bread. . . ." Or he might pretend to be a helpless old woman who is being maltreated and made fun of by some nasty boys. So then you'll come to her rescue. You'll think you came to the rescue of an old woman, but it was Jesus Christ himself. When you feed someone who is hungry, give a drink to the thirsty, comfort to the suffering, help to the weak, support to those who stumble, when you lend a hand with someone's work or warm someone who is cold . . . it is just the same as if you did all that to Jesus Christ. He sees and knows it all, but when you stand up at Judgement Day and they start judging you for all the bad things you did . . . '

'Ah, but I won't do anything bad . . . '

'Don't speak too soon. Life is long. The cunning tempter is always next to you, whispering in your ear and giving you bad ideas. You'll hold out for a bit and then you'll give in. You'll offend someone or you'll be too lazy to do something that should be done or, Lord forbid, you'll tell a lie or deceive someone or, Lord forbid, you'll take something that isn't yours or hit another person or even just a cat. . . . Well, you'll get up to enough nasty, wicked things in your life. . . . And so, when you stand up on Judgement Day and they start judging you for all the bad things you have done, the Lord will smile at you and say: "I know this lad. When I was hungry he gave me a piece of bread, when I was thirsty he gave me some water, when I was being badly treated he came to my aid, when I was drowning in the river he held out his hand to me, when I was carrying a heavy load he helped me, when I was stumbling he held me up. . . . This is a good boy, his place is in heaven." You will say to him: "Lord! But I have never seen you before!" The Lord will disagree with you and say: "No, you have often seen me. You went to the rescue of an old woman, but it was I, you gave water to a thirsty man, but it was I, you gave alms to a beggar-woman, but it was I. . . ."'

'The Lord', my mother would continue, 'sees your every step and even knows what you are thinking. He sees the good things and the bad. So you just try to do only good things. Your guardian angel is standing at your right shoulder and you mustn't upset him. Whenever you do anything good, he is overjoyed. He laughs and smiles. But the Devil behind your left shoulder furrows his brow and writhes about when this happens. And when you do something bad, the Devil will snigger and rub his hands. Why should you make the Devil happy like that?'

Given that Stepanida Ivanovna was seventeen when she married (her husband, the twenty-seven-year-old widower, Aleksey Alekseevich, already had two children on his hands), then, at a rough estimate, Stepanida Ivanovna got up in the dark, before anyone else, in order to light the stove, cook food and see to the animals and other domestic chores somewhere around twenty thousand times. But the first thing she did was pray. Still only half dressed, in her white night-dress, on her knees before the flame of the icon-lamp that lit the icons in their special place in the far corner, she whispered those twenty thousand ardent, heartfelt morning prayers, accompanying them with deep sighs, whilst everyone was still asleep and before she started to clatter about with oven prongs and cast-iron pots. Twenty thousand quiet conversations with God, conversations whispered on her knees, accompanied by deep sighs, twenty thousand requests and entreaties, twenty thousand expressions of praise and thanks. But the main thing, evidently, was her sense of unity with God, or merging with him heart and soul, so that she finished each prayer with tears in her eyes and a feeling of peace and joy which every time emerged in the form of one and the same phrase, formula and culmination: 'Glory to thee, O Lord, glory to thee.'

Twenty thousand prayers – that was in the morning. Add to them as many again in the evening before bedtime. When I was tiny I would still be soundly and sweetly asleep in the small hours before dawn (except that I might sometimes happen to half open my eyes for a second as I turned over and the semi-darkness of the house, the flame of the icon-lamp in front of the icons and my mother on her knees in her white night-dress would imprint themselves on my mind, as if suddenly photographed). Yet when it came to evening prayers my mother would frequently have me stand next to her. Also on my knees and crossing myself, also whispering something (although in all probability not a whole complicated prayer, but some prayer-like phrase consisting of two or three words or so), I rather listened to Mother's whispering than prayed myself but, just the same, a delightful sweetness filled the soul of this child, so much so that he experienced spasms in the throat, a rush of warmth to the heart and tears in his eyes. Sometimes, however (and such moments were particularly sweet), I would turn, as I said, from side to side in bed, half open my eyes for a moment and then, overcoming my sleepiness (which is not easily done in childhood) and the warmth of the bed, I would get up and kneel down next to my mother. Those morning prayers (perhaps in part because they were, after all, associated with sacrifice and self-discipline) were especially sweet and the evening prayers could not bear comparison to them. Apart from that, the cares of the day did not leave you completely by evening and had to be overcome, there would still be circles on the mirror-like surface of one's soul, like those that appear on water when someone throws some pebbles in. They do not disappear immediately, for the clean, smooth expanse of water needs time to calm down and grow still, but in the morning . . . in the morning everything is quiet and peaceful and you yourself (four or five years old) are almost an angel.

Can you imagine this picture? A woman and a little child are kneeling in the semi-darkness of a peasant house before the icon-lamp, its light is falling on the icons and they are deep in prayer. . . .

It was thanks to my mother that I already knew a good many Bible stories by that time, stories that she told me in simplified versions which I was the more easily able to understand. There was Joseph's dream (the seven fat cows and seven lean ones)[21] and the building of the Tower of Babel ('They wanted to build a tower such as would enable them to reach God, but God confused their tongues. One says "Bring me nails" and his fellow brings him clay, another says "Bring me a hammer" and his fellow brings him a jug of water. They thus had no success.') There was Lot's wife who was turned into a pillar of salt because she could not resist looking towards Sodom and Gomorrah as they burned, and the judgement of Solomon in the case of the two women who were arguing over a child, and the good Samaritan who helped the injured man on the road; and of course the story of Jesus Christ was told me more than once with particular conviction and detail.

On top of that we happened to have a unique set of picture cards in the house. (By a strange trick of fate, despite the fact that nothing now remains of the old house, of its way of life, everyday routine, utensils, furniture, crockery, clothes or of any other single object connected with it, those cards have survived, although probably not all of them.) I am going through them at this moment. They are frayed at the edges and creased so badly that the two pieces hardly hang together. The cards have yellow margins on which something is written in various languages: French, Russian, English, Greek and Hebrew, and on some there is Italian as well. They are clearly numbered in the lower right-hand corner, although the numbers in the set as it has survived are irregular: 2, 4, 7, 18, 39, 43, 60. . . . They do not go beyond 60 (twenty-five of them have survived in all), and No. 60 is for some reason 'The Earthly Paradise', which is really the one which should come at the beginning of the set. Well, it is a tree with a broad, reddish coloured, knotty trunk, under which sit Adam and Eve, naked. There is a lake nearby, more trees, there are hanging vines and grazing animals: a giraffe, an elephant, a goat and a crane. Perhaps it is a lion cub at Adam and Eve's feet. In general the cards are executed in a manner that combines an element of conventionality and primitiveness with the authenticity of a photograph. For example, where the towns of Jaffa or Nablus are pictured (Sychar or Shechem), despite all the stylistic simplification, you believe that every house shown really existed there, in that very place and with those very windows. In the case of Mount Tabor, the road that wound up from its base to its rounded summit had exactly those zigzags and the tiny monastery at the top exactly that silhouette, although, when you begin to think about the proportions, the road in the picture would in reality be I do not know how wide, quite possibly something like the Volga. Here we have 'The Last Supper', 'The Church of St Mary Magdalene', 'The Tomb of the Saviour', 'The Bearing of the Cross', 'The Deposition from the Cross', 'The Mocking of the Saviour', 'The Entombment', 'The Prayer Concerning the Cup' and 'The Garden of Gethsemane', the latter shown with an ancient oak in the middle of the picture. There is one further inscription in Russian on each of the cards: 'With the Blessing of the Holy City of Jerusalem.'

Grandfather also had a small coral cross with a tiny

piece of glass at the centre. If you shut one eye and looked, you suddenly saw, unexpectedly enlarged, as if by a miracle, that very same oak in the Garden of Gethsemane.

I had no doubts as to the reality of what occurred in the Holy Land in biblical times nor concerning everything that happened to Jesus Christ, no doubts and not even the shadow of a doubt.

Of all the external rituals to which Stepanida Ivanovna accustomed me, first and foremost came fasts of various kinds and preparations for Confession and Communion. Not eating dairy and meat products was not so difficult in those days, since Father deliberately went to Vladimir before, say, Lent (with Golubchik harnessed to a low, wide sleigh), and upon his return took out from beneath the pile of clover huge (or perhaps they only seemed huge to me then?) frozen pike-perch, fat dried roach, tins (of sturgeon in tomato – I do not think anything in the world could have tasted better than the contents of those tins, probably because they had been produced in town and not at home in the country), herrings (fat Caspian herrings) and dried fruit. We might have found a few dried apples of our own, but the prunes, raisins and dried apricots, as well as the dried pears from which we made extremely tasty pear kvass, Father brought from Vladimir along with the frozen fish. The oil, you will recall, was virtually our own ('Lenya, take a look through the window and see if Grigory Ivanovich's windmill is working'), just as were our various stocks of mushrooms. The honey (remember), was also ours. Steamed cabbage, thick pea soup, carrot, turnip and potato pies, mushroom soup with noodles, frozen apples (which have a waxen appearance, but when they thaw they go dark brown, soft and succulent, and their skin comes away on its own), sauerkraut, salted cucumbers (with potatoes), beetroot . . . all that (not forgetting the frozen pike-perch and the rest) made the lenten fast virtually unnoticeable. Well, we would miss a hot flapjack with milk or a soft-boiled egg, but that was all trivial. If the truth be told, I do not remember any sense of suffering or torture during Lent. On the other hand, I well remember Christmas Eve, when it was forbidden to eat anything at all throughout the whole day until the appearance of the first star.

No matter how short the winter day might be, if you had not even had breakfast you would run yourself off your feet, dashing out into the street from the onset of dusk to see if the first star, however feeble, was visible. It was wonderful if the sky was the clear sky that appears at the end of a frosty, sunny winter's day, when at any moment not some faint little star but whole handfuls of stars, whole cascades of them would appear and adorn the heavens with diamonds. If, on the other hand, it was overcast and a snowstorm was blowing, or overcast because of soft snow, gently falling, or if it were simply overcast with neither a snowstorm nor an ordinary snowfall, it was left entirely up to Mother to decide whether the first star had appeared in the gloomy mass of cloud, or rather beyond the gloomy mass of cloud, and whether we had the right to break our fast. I do not think Stepanida Ivanovna ever kept me fasting artificially long – indeed, the opposite was much more likely the case.

And what, then, happened after the moment when the star finally appeared? Ah! There are no words to express it. Special pancakes for stuffing (a cross between ordinary pancakes and flapjacks, thinner than the latter but as big as a good-sized pancake – that is, big enough to cover a plate) would be cooked in advance, along with peas (not soup, not some sort of gruel or pea-flavoured liquid, but whole boiled peas). You would put some peas on one of the special pancakes, roll it up and then eat it with the peas inside, washing it all down with kvass and only kvass. Oh, oh and oh again!

During the days of fasting and confession I had to be sure not to listen to the whisperings of the Cunning One, the Devil who would stand behind my left shoulder and tempt me to break the fast and secretly down some nice, forbidden titbit. The tempter sat right in front of me in the form of my elder brother, Nikolay. When I was, say, five, he was all of sixteen, so of course he had been to school, to a Soviet school, having first attended the rural primary school for four years and then Cherkutino SYP (School for the Youth of the Peasantry – for some reason that combination of letters makes me shudder as if I had inadvertently touched a rat). He had either already left this school or was just about to leave and so his brains were already half frozen, anaesthetized, sterilized, half stuffed with the vulgar, cheap but, alas, effective and ubiquitous propaganda of the time. There in school he had joined the circle of militant atheists. Well, he did not get much of a chance to be militant in our house. Grandfather, Aleksey Dmitrievich, was still alive and my father, Aleksey Alekseevich, had still not been frightened by the coming reforms (as he was to be a couple of years later), and you would not put up much of a fight against those two. Nevertheless, I think I am right in saying that there were some attempts at iconoclasm on Nikolay's part and that he once tried to carry virtually all the icons up to the attic but, I should emphasize, these efforts were unsuccessful if not pitiful. However, as I now understand, a certain status quo had been established. My parents would not have allowed Nikolay to do anything at home, but not only did they do nothing to prevent the school bringing up this young atheist, they did not even make the slightest effort by way of spiritual or educational guidance or instruction to oppose the process. (The same thing was to happen in my case when I went to school two or three years later.)

And so I, a lad of four or five whose mother trained him in prayer, fasting and confession, became the chief object of attention and field of activity for the militant atheist, Nikolay. First, with me actually looking on, he would eat things which were forbidden to me, showing obvious relish and champing demonstratively. Secondly, when he saw that I was particularly hungry, he would say. 'Hey, Vovka! A hot rye fritter with milk would be just the thing now. . . . Or a buttered pancake. Or how about putting your finger into the jar of soured cream? Come on, now! I know where the jar of soured cream is, come on!'

I must say that not once did I succumb to temptation at such moments and that in those days not a single snigger was uttered behind my left shoulder – at least, not in connection with the events described.

Of course I was also taken to church. The transition from my rural, so to speak, entourage – peasant houses, animal stalls, paths, grassy expanses, Russian stoves, low ceilings, benches (cluttered with kitchen utensils), horse-collars, sheepskin coats and paraffin lamps (with half-inch wicks) – the transition from all that to the stone church with its ornamental paved floor, its candelabra which burned bright with the light of dozens of candles, with its flashing candlesticks, carved and gilded iconostasis, its dome which somehow seemed like a second sky, its bright murals on the walls, must have been a transition into another world, into another dimension, as they would say now; but if I limit myself to what I remember, to what I actually remember, rather than fill out my impressions on the basis of later experience, then all that remains in my memory from my very earliest years is the sensation of warm oil as the cross was made on my forehead (that is, during the rite of Unction), and the warm, sweet taste of wine from a small silver spoon during Communion.

But now I must write about something I cannot omit, although I find the task practically impossible. This must have happened a few years later than the early infancy I have been describing. I was certainly already going to school (and, consequently, was no longer going with my mother to church). I would no doubt be seven or eight years old. We Alepino lads liked to play different games in the church grounds and even in the church porch. Moreover, the older boys, almost young men, along with the adolescents and youngsters, all gathered there together. Perhaps we did not play absolutely every time, preferring to meet and simply sit talking in the church porch.

The older boys would talk among themselves or make little home-made guns (loaded with powdered match-heads instead of gunpowder), or they might discuss a raid on someone's orchard or arrange to go to the forest the next day and bake potatoes in the coals of a bonfire, and we little ones would be there listening, not taking part in the older lads' conversation and certainly not interfering in what they were doing. The older boys might amuse themselves by setting us young ones against each other so that a fight broke out, or they might sit in the church porch and make whistles from willow or bird-cherry twigs in which the sap had just settled after the spring. There was plenty to do. . . .

Now then, I remember a period (let me emphasize that this did not happen on one evening only) when we would sit like that in the church porch as the darkness gathered and the twilight turned into a warm evening and I would suddenly feel an irresistible urge to go into the church and remain there the whole night. The church had a heavy padlock, of course, and it would have been totally impossible to get inside and, naturally, it would have been frightening for a little lad to be in the church at night, but I had an *irresistible urge* to go in and stay there. I had the feeling that there, inside the nocturnal church, someone *loved me very much and was waiting eagerly for me*. I had the feeling that, if I stayed the night in the church, it would be a sweet and wonderful experience such as would never happen outside. There I am loved very much and eagerly awaited, but I cannot go there, I have to be here, with the boys.

Reader, imagine that gang of village boys sitting in the darkened church porch. That is not hard to do; but imagine now that one of them, a really – dare I say it? – snotty-nosed kid, has the urge to go into the church at night and stay there all night because he is apparently loved there very much and eagerly awaited. . . .

Did this faceless 'loved and awaited' ever take on the

100

concrete image of the Mother of God or of Jesus Christ? I no longer remember. I do not know. I remember only the feeling that I was loved very much and eagerly awaited there.

10

MY MOTHER WOULD FREQUENTLY EXCLAIM: 'THERE NOW, and you said God doesn't exist!' It does not matter that I never tried to convince her that there was no God. She evidently thought that everyone around her took that view. Most likely, though, she resorted to her pet expression – 'There now, and you said God doesn't exist!' – whenever she saw the results of her prayers in real life or the workings of Divine Providence manifesting themselves even beyond her expectations, without really thinking anything.

I told her, for instance, about an episode that involved our platoon. We were in summer camp at the time in the village of Novaya Kupavna, a village that stretched out along both sides of the main road from Moscow to Gorky, about thirty-three kilometres from Moscow. After the rest-hour (a nap after lunch), our platoon set off for a place where instruction in hand-to-hand fighting was to be given. The platoon was being led by Sergeant-Major Karasenko, a Ukrainian with a fine resonant voice. We were marching along the edge of the Gorky road, carrying fascines (for bayoneting) and dummy rifles with bayonets (so as not to spoil real rifles and bayonets). We were marching in a column four deep, each section itself forming a column. Our section, the fourth, was on the left, nearest of all to the asphalt, along the join between the asphalt and the land to the side of the road, you could say. Our section (company mortar gunners) contained a few more people than the rest. There were, we shall say, nine or ten people in the others, whereas ours had fourteen. The result was that whenever the platoon was arranged in a column four deep, each section itself forming a column, our left-hand column would have a 'tail' four persons longer than the rest. Usually the command would come: 'Fourth section, disperse.' That meant that our 'tail' had to spread itself across the other three columns so that the platoon acquired the correct rectangular formation with no tail. We 'dispersed' on this particular occasion too. I had been marching along last of all, right at the back, and so I moved over from the far left to the far right, from the column nearest the asphalt to the one nearest the ditch.

We were marching along, still feeling sluggish and sleepy. The after-dinner rest-hour is short, you just have time to get warm and relaxed when the command rings out: 'Company, on your feet!'

Sergeant-Major Karasenko was the first to recover from this feeling of sluggishness. He gave the command: 'Sing!'

Our singing leader began, but also somehow sluggishly and without gusto, so that you did not even feel like joining in.

'Now then!' Sergeant-Major Karasenko scolded us. 'That's hardly the way to start up a song', and he began to sing himself, his voice ringing out high, sonorous and full of vigour. A second more and we would all have joined together in a loud rendition of the song and then, perhaps, what happened in the following instant would not have happened: our song would probably have awakened the driver.

I should mention that as we marched along the side of the road an endless column of many hundreds of heavy Studebakers was passing by, engulfing us in gusts of hot air and intermittent noise; and so, just as we were about to take up the song, the next Studebaker to come along ploughed into the lines of our platoon. They were going from the front somewhere east (presumably to be loaded with military supplies) and the youthful driver had fallen asleep at the wheel. Sergeant-Major Karasenko was struck by the front of the vehicle, the radiator (he was walking farthest to the left, along the edge of the asphalt). Our section was mown down to a man by the right side of the vehicle, and the first person to be mown down would have been me, had I remained at the back and not moved across to the right-hand column.

When Stepanida Ivanovna heard the story of what happened she shouted out, raising her eyes to heaven: 'And you say that God doesn't exist!'

I recall another incident as well, but at this point I must digress.

Our family tree had yet one more branch, an unusual, romantic and exotic one. Evidently my father's brother, Mikhail Alekseevich, was a man with a romantic streak. I think he even wrote poetry, although, I am sorry to say not a single line remains of it. He had a collection of stones, which for a peasant in a village was rare indeed. However, I said above that the top layer of the Russian peasantry was, even in the years before the Revolution, sending fresh sap-filled shoots up into the higher Russian cultural stratum – the intelligentsia.

Our forest, Samoylovsky Forest by name, is intersected by deep gullies, along which brooklets of spring water run into the River Eza, which is also in the forest. It was in the beds of these gullies and along the Eza itself that Mikhail Alekseevich used to search out and gather his rare stones, fossilized freshwater corals and all kinds of other fossils. Later, when Mikhail Alekseevich no longer frequented our area or our house, a basket full of these stones was still to be seen standing in our attic. Only one exhibit remains from his entire collection and not because it was preserved in the attic but because I hit it with my spade whilst planting a cherry tree where our yard used to be. This stone (which actually is a fossilized freshwater coral) is on my desk in my Moscow apartment.

Mikhail Alekseevich served (as they said in those days) on the railway as something between a ticket-collector and an inspector. Looking at a surviving photograph of him in the company of his fellow-railwaymen, you could take them – from their appearance, dress and dignified expressions – to be, say, bank managers, actors from the Imperial Theatre or presidents of various countries all gathered together.

Despite this respectable appearance Mikhail Alekseevich fell in love with a young Ukrainian girl from Poltava whom he happened to meet. I say 'despite', as the Ukrainian girl was obviously just an ordinary local lass and they spent the whole of the rest of their lives in Poltava, living in a modest little white house or, to be exact, clay-walled cottage. Her name was Tatyana. They had a son called Zhenya, a handsome fellow (judging by the photograph), as often happens when there is a mixture of nationalities, even if extremely closely related ones. He was in the air force and was killed at the very beginning of the war. When our forces retreated, they did not blow up the bridge in Kalinin in time and tried desperately to bomb it when it was too late. Well, the Germans of course made a good job of defending it. It was in the air over this bridge that Evgeny Mikhailovich Soloukhin, the handsome young man from Poltava, perished along with many, many others.

(By an irony of fate I later found myself, as a champion of things ancient, defending this old and beautiful bridge – the pride of the former Tver – from the Kalinin authorities who had made up their minds to demolish it.)

But we have jumped too far ahead in time. In the last years before the Revolution and in the first years after it our family simply knew that somewhere in Poltava, in a clay-walled cottage, lived Uncle Misha; but, to a little village lost among the Vladimir countryside, Poltava[22] no doubt seemed far, far away, at the end of the earth and naturally my father would never make it there with Golubchik, not as he would visit Uncle Sasha in Peksha.

In the first years after the Revolution the Bolsheviks, having seized power in the country, took all the grain away from the peasants in order to keep hold of that power. That was called the Food-Supply Policy. The aim was to concentrate all the grain in their own hands and then distribute it as they saw fit, thus keeping the population in a state of submission. Famine spread throughout the country. This is what Stepanida Ivanovna told me:

'I used up the remaining handful of flour, there was none left and no way of lasting out until the new grain appeared. But there were the children to think of. Well, you had not yet arrived. Maria had only just been born, Victor was three, Nikolay was six, Katyusha eleven, Valentina twelve, Tonya thirteen, Klavdia fifteen. So many mouths. . . . Well, they would have something to eat that day, but what about the next? The next day they would want to eat again. Suddenly, we saw some strangers riding through the village. They were in three drays. They stopped at our house and asked: "Where does 'leksey Soloukhin live?"

'"Here."

'Then they threw down two sacks of flour from one of the drays.

'"This is for you from Poltava."

'"What do you mean?"

'"It's simple enough. We went to the Ukraine for flour and someone on the outskirts of Poltava asked us where we were from."

'"We're from Vladimir Province," we said.

'"Have you heard of a village called Alepino?"

'"Have we heard of it? It's only twenty versts from our village. We'll be passing through Alepino."

'"Well, the man asked us to take two sacks of flour for 'leksey Soloukhin. It seems he's 'leksey's brother, is that right?"

'"Yes, yes . . . "

'"So, here you are, we've brought them."

'We made it to the time when the new grain appeared,' my mother would say and then add, raising her eyes to heaven, 'and you say God doesn't exist.'

And, you have to admit, a great many things came together here. On that critical last day, the day despair was about to set in, two sacks of flour arrive from mysterious Poltava to be dumped on the grass outside your house. The men had gone all the way to Poltava in their carts, but then of course they were noticed by Mikhail Alekseevich, he got talking to them (there were of course any number of peasants travelling in horse-drawn carts), decided to trust them and they agreed to take the two sacks (with a horse and cart every pound weighs heavy on such a long journey and, naturally, it would have been better for them if they had loaded up with another two sackfuls for themselves), and then they went across half the Ukraine and half Russia and did not make off with the flour (yet who was going to check on them or on what they did and when?) and, finally, they passed our house on the very day that the last handful of flour was used up. . . .

Coincidences, chance, conscience, they are all here, but here too (possibly Stepanida Ivanovna was right after all) we see the workings of Divine Providence.

11

I HAVE ALREADY MENTIONED SOMEWHERE IN THESE SKETCHES of mine that all the Soloukhins had dark hair (white teeth), dark eyes, curly locks and straight noses, whereas all the Cheburovs (my mother's side of the family) had hair like straw, noses like potatoes and light-blue eyes.

Aleksey Alekseevich was a real Soloukhin. I should say that, unlike the Cheburovs, the Soloukhins never became fat with the approach of old age, but retained their wiriness, if you can talk of wiriness in relation to thickset (though tall), big-boned men endowed with more than average physical strength.

As is well known, the shafts are fixed to a wide, low sleigh by means of stout ropes of a particular type tied in a special knot. These ropes are called tugs. In freezing temperatures these tugs turn as hard as rock. Well, should one of the tugs snap, Aleksey Alekseevich would work it in his hands until the water flowed out of it – this was at thirty degrees below, or at any rate at more than twenty – and tie it up in a new knot, after which it would go as hard as rock again.

Strange as it may seem, I remember this following mannerism of his just about better than any other: if, whilst we were having dinner (or breakfast or supper or, in a word, a meal) he needed to say something, everyone would fall silent (because he was about to answer or speak), and he would slowly and diligently chew whatever he had in his mouth until it had completely disappeared and only then would he answer or say what he wanted.

He did everything else just as slowly and diligently. Whenever we had pancakes my mother would place a big pile of them on the table on a single plate. They would be large enough to cover the whole plate. Only the head of the household was allowed to cut the pancakes at table – that is, the selfsame Aleksey Alekseevich. First he would move the plate of pancakes closer to himself, then, securing them with a fork, he would cut them in half (along the diameter, you could say), after which he would unhurriedly give the plate a quarter turn and once again cut the pile in half. Thus the pancakes would be cut into four, the plate would be returned to the centre of the table and all of us at table (and there were many of us) would begin to eat them, being careful to take exactly one-quarter each. If you laid hold of two-quarters at once you would be repaid with a blow from a wooden spoon on your forehead. This act could be performed not only by Aleksey Alekseevich but by Grandfather, Aleksey Dmitrievich, who had a sturdy spoon made of maple with which he could reach the most distant parts of the table.

One thing that Aleksey Alekseevich did especially slowly and diligently was to secure the load on the cart before a long journey, although in those days there could be no particularly long journeys. I should imagine that Aleksey Alekseevich never ventured farther than Vladimir (forty versts away) with his Golubchik. I have already spoken about the visits to Peksha (now the town of Kolchugino). Apart from that, there would be trips to the station. Our railway station was Undol, situated twenty-five versts from Alepino. A number of my sisters were already living in Moscow, my mother would go and stay with them (moreover, my mother's sister, Aunt Katya Polunina, had also long since been a Muscovite), and my sisters themselves might come to the village to spend their holidays in summer, after which they would need to go back. On each of these occasions Golubchik would have to be harnessed and driven to the station. You can tell what the traffic was like in our parts then: impatient for the guests to arrive, we would clamber on to the bell-tower and look out in the direction they might come from. We would catch sight of the shaft-bow and then the horse amongst the tall rye whilst they were still two or three kilometres away from the village: 'They're coming, they're coming!' Home we run as fast as we can to tell Mother, so that she can prepare the samovar.

My father had no special line of work of the kind that is frequently combined with peasant labour. For there were peasants who at the same time were carpenters, joiners, stove-makers, saddlers, slaughterers (of cattle), roofers, sawyers (cutting logs into planks), I could go on and on. . . . Aleksey Alekseevich performed none of these special peasant tasks, he was simply a peasant, that is, a ploughman, a mower, a woodcutter, but more than anything else he was Golubchik's driver. I am not referring here to the fact that he used Golubchik to carry sheaves and hay and firewood and straw and everything else that has to be carried on a peasant farm, but to the fact that he liked travelling more than anything else on earth. Probably his first journeys came about because those circular cakes of clean yellow wax which I have already described in one chapter of these sketches – the product of our small wax-maker's business – had to be taken to Vladimir.

The raw material for the wax-maker's was also required – the old combs. It is possible that in searching out the combs he had to roam about in remote places with Golubchik. There was also the trip to Karavaevo on Assumption Day. There were trips to the fairs at Yuryev-Polsky and Kuzmin Monastery, to markets and simply to the town for various things. In one way or another Aleksey Alekseevich travelled about more than any other single peasant in our village. You could say that all the others, compared with him, were stay-at-homes. He never urged the horse on by using his whip, although it was always at hand where it could be seen. No, the horse went at his own pace, so that a journey which could take a few hours would last a whole day. Evidently it was not the aim of the journey that was important to Father so much as the very process of travelling, the road itself, the rattle of the cart (or squeak of the sleigh), the slow procession of copses and villages, flat fields with bushes in them and gentle hills; the whole unspectacular landscape which was our dear home was the important thing and, even more so, the solitude.

It looks as though Aleksey Alekseevich placed the proverb 'More haste, less speed' above everything else. In fact, I remember a number of proverbs that my father liked using, each of which represented a whole sphere of peasant life as it was then. Well, 'More haste, less speed' – that one was not so much a common saying as a commonplace. Here is something he used to like to say when the occasion presented itself: 'When the horse collars clatter, the horses can't sleep.' Here you must imagine those sweetest hours of sleep before dawn when the inevitability of an early start would reach my consciousness, even though I might be still half asleep, because people were already moving in the house and, although no one had wakened me or disturbed me as yet, I already knew that they would in a few minutes time and that everything had been agreed the previous evening: we were to be up early for a journey or work in the fields, in other words: 'When the horse collars clatter, the horses can't sleep.'

He also liked to repeat, whenever he made a good job of something as only a peasant could, even if it was just nailing two boards together to mend a stall: 'Whoever tries to pull this down, will start swearing.'

Again, I am not going to speak about sayings such as 'Bread does not run after the stomach' or 'Seven don't wait for one', sayings that my father would use frequently but which are quite common. Here, however, is one I have not heard since from anyone: 'Your stomach is worse than your neighbour at remembering a good turn.' That is, however much you please it and feed it today, it will soon ask for more food. When my turn to be an adolescent arrived, say when I was thirteen or fourteen, and I and other adolescent boys (together with a few ringleaders who were a little older than us) got down to 'arranging' for a bottle on a feast-day, if only one between all of us (frying some eggs on a fire in the forest and drinking the contents of the bottle), Father sensed the age I had reached and, with all the guests around the table looking on, suddenly took to pouring out a glass for me along with everyone else. As he did so he would be sure to say: 'Drink at the table and not behind the stable.'

He liked a drink himself and had a stock of his own alcoholic cordials made with lemon peel, cherries (more often than not) and rowan-tree berries. I could be wrong about the last one. There surely must have been some of that as well, because the orchard was full of Nezhin rowan trees, but I have no mental picture of a cordial made from rowan-tree berries, whereas I well remember cherries in the empty decanter, even if simply because we would furtively help ourselves to those intoxicating cherries and eat them. On feast-days, especially if we were guests in somebody's house, Aleksey Alekseevich was capable of getting tight. Doubtless he did so on feast-days at home too, but I do not remember this as it would not be so noticeable. What would happen at home? He would get drunk, lie down and go to sleep. If we were guests somewhere, though, we would have to get home with Golubchik and, despite being very small, I still had a very uncomfortable feeling: will we make it? Will we turn over? Will Golubchik find the way back himself? And no doubt my mother shouted at Father whenever this happened, because I remember drunken feast-days in other people's houses better than those spent at home. When on the following day my mother would continue nagging Aleksey Alekseevich (Lenya) about what had happened the day before, he would be sure to turn it all into a joke by saying: 'You can't be glorified without miracles.'

His frequent journeys with Golubchik – usually he did not return the same day, but two or three days and nights later – meant that Aleksey Alekseevich had friends in all directions radiating out from Alepino – that is, on the roads to Yuryev-Polsky, Vladimir, Undol, Petushki, Peksha and Karavaevo. These were the people he would call on in order to spend the night. In Nerazh, a village in the forest, he had a friend who, by the way, was a keen hunter, at Undol station itself he had a friend called Kroshkin and another one near the bridge over the Koloksha. In accordance with some unwritten rule of friendship Aleksey Alekseevich would drop by on these mates at any hour of the day or night, expecting to spend the night, just as if he had gone home. I would sometimes be with him when he called on those friends of his, since I too spent plenty of hours, day and night, with my father in the sleigh or cart, travelling along both winter and summer roads.

When the collective farm was set up (an event I have described in greater detail elsewhere), they took Golubchik away, along with all the other peasants' horses, and put him in a communal barn, or rather a big shed. People are used to not thinking about this monstrous act, but I must repeat what I have said previously. Supposing they were to say to our modern city-dwellers – Muscovites – that tomorrow they must put all their dogs, large and small, into one common doghouse! Well now, what a wave of outrage, protest, indignation, complaints and tears there would be; but it is not dogs and cats we are talking about here, but a horse – your provider and even your best friend.

In the early days the peasants would call by the communal barn in order to see their horses. They would bring some titbits with them to supplement the grub provided by the collective farm. So, Father was once seeing to the food in Golubchik's manger when Golubchik grabbed his hand in a frenzy and tore all the skin off the back of it. Why he did this remains a mystery; but not so long ago I was talking about it with one of our fine Russian writers and he immediately realized what had happened:

'Of course Golubchik did it to your father for betraying him. How could he know that it was forced on him, that Bolsheviks were involved and so on? He decided that your father betrayed him by handing him over to the communal barn. . . .'

Well now, it is not impossible that this fine Russian writer was right.

Father lived for more than thirty-five years after collectivization. For all that time, whilst his strength lasted, he worked on the collective farm just like all the other Alepino peasants, but it was life by inertia rather than real life. The same thing at home. At first we kept a cow and some sheep, but after that we changed to a goat. Things gradually began to get neglected, to collapse and wear out; the interest in life had gone. Of all the many sayings and repeated phrases that my father habitually used the one we heard most often now was 'It's all right, we shan't go without firewood', spoken in answer to Stepanida Ivanovna's tedious daily demands, the point being that every day, in an attempt to prepare for the fast approaching winter, if nothing more, Stesha would nag her Lenya: 'Lenya, what are you lying there for? Winter is just round the corner and there are only two sticks of firewood left. What will we heat the stove with? Lenya, we need firewood.'

'It's all right, we shan't go without firewood.'

Somehow or other, then, whether it meant taking down a stall, shortening the barn attached to the house or bringing firewood from the forest at the last moment, somehow or other Russia's peasants, Alepino's old men and women, finished their days, living by inertia a somnolent, uninteresting, tasteless life. 'It's all right, we shan't go without firewood.'

12

SO THEN, A CERTAIN ETERNAL SUBSTANCE, REFERRED TO IN the course of our earthly, human existence as the soul, found itself installed in a tiny body with straw-coloured hair and light-blue eyes, a body that was easily wounded, easily hurt, mortal, but which was also receptive to all earthly pleasures and joys. Those same eyes became the two windows, openings or observation slits through which, looking round at its new abode (the earth), this chance settler gazed out upon all the world's beauties and horrors. At first it looked at everything around with the eyes of a baby, then with those of a little boy, then with those of an adolescent. Now they are a sixty-year-old man's eyes, somewhat faded and puffy and half covered with tired lids, but, just the same, at times an attentive observer will once more catch in those eyes a fleeting glimpse of that pure blue which was there in the eyes of the seven-to-ten-year-old, a glimpse of his artlessness and curiosity, rapture and horror, bewilderment and delight: a glimpse of the child.

And so it was that, alongside the golden dandelion, the round white cloud floating across the dark-blue sky, the lily of the valley beneath the shady fir, the icon lamp before the icons, the bright water flowing down the river (a yellow water-lily upon it with a blue dragon-fly atop), alongside my mother's kind world and the beautiful face of my sister, there suddenly appeared in the world the monstrous, ugly, inexplicable cruelty of other people. And when this happened, where were *their* souls? After all, they too each had two eyes that also served as openings, observation slits and windows on the world. Why did I become a voluntary or involuntary witness to a great many ugly acts of cruelty? I shall talk about two such acts, if no more, acts which, however, will very likely appear insignificant, primitive and trifling when seen against the background of other things I was unable to see, or know about, but which were going on at the time throughout the land. We shall not speak of those things for the present.

I do not, though, consider certain of my father's actions as examples of cruelty, any more than I do the fact that he made me take part in them whilst I was still very small. We lived a workaday peasant life and I, a peasant lad, had to be taught everything about it. What use would I have been if I had grown up still a peasant, but unable, or unwilling, to slaughter a sheep?

Yes, Father would make me hold a sheep by its front and hind legs which, by the way, would be prudently tied together, whilst he pulled its head back and cut its defenceless throat with a sharp knife, something he did without a great deal of skill (he was not, of course, a professional slaughterer). The sheep would jerk about in my little hands until the jerking gradually subsided and the animal finally became quite motionless; but I would still feel its eye turned towards me, specifically me rather than the chief protagonist, and a look of bewilderment seemed to remain fixed in that eye: 'Well, him I can understand, he's a grown peasant, he can do it if he wants to, but what are you doing? Why did you have to do that? It was the last thing I expected of you. . . .'

We even slaughtered a piglet. We did it badly, with Father repeatedly poking his knife deep inside the piglet from a place under its left leg. Evidently failing to find the piglet's heart first time, he tried stabbing at various spots there in the depths and the piglet emitted blood-curdling squeals, but in the end it too gradually went quiet and, again, a look of bewilderment remained fixed in its small but expressive (damn it) piggy eye

No, it is other details from my childhood that I have in

mind now, although the way I remember them may seem comical, since I do not simply recall them but still experience all the pain they caused me then, when I was probably five.

It was an August day and threshing was in progress. This last point I know because the roomy, cool threshing-barn, containing the horse-driven threshing-mill, was open (this all happened before the collective farm was established). Perhaps, though, they were still only bringing the sheaves into the shed and the actual threshing had not yet begun. A squirrel had been discovered in an old and leafy or, better, spreading white willow with a huge rounded crown. I do not know why she had run into the village from the firs and pines of the nearby wood; but the small boys, the bigger lads and perhaps even some of the adults raised the cry: 'A squirrel! A squirrel! A squirrel!' Immediately sticks and stones started flying towards her. She jumped across from the first willow to another, but there they ended. It is true that there were orchards and kitchen gardens in which she could easily have vanished, especially as the entire gang of people would not have run after her there, but the little woodland animal, in a terrible fright, and doubtless feeling unsure of herself in the village, raced off along the ground until she was finally driven into the threshing-barn, where she crouched right up near the roof, beneath a cross-beam. Well, the question has to be asked: what was all the urgency for? A polecat would have been different, a polecat steals chickens (although I might mention that, in the long run, it does more good than harm to the peasants); had it been a mouse or a rat – which a peasant never misses the opportunity of killing – then everything would have been fine, but here they were dealing with nothing more than an innocent little squirrel with a bushy tail, pretty face and equally pretty front paws. What did all those youths and boys want with her when they surrounded her and drove her into the shed, continuing with their senseless amusement there, in the shed? One of the youths started to poke and knock at a chink beneath the cross-beam where the squirrel had taken refuge, and in an instant my child's consciousness fixed for the rest of my life, like a photograph, the sight of that little face covered in blood, with the drops of red falling down from beneath the cross-beam on to the dusty earthen floor of the shed.

I remember how, after that small, senseless tragedy, I ran off to a secluded spot in our orchard and cried there longer and more bitterly than perhaps at any other time before or since. At that moment I hated all adults (and there had been a great many adults there, although perhaps they had taken no part in the hounding of the poor little animal, but they had been present) and, I remember, since I had no other way of making my protest (perhaps, in fact, I was no more than four at the time!), I made this strange promise to myself, something in the nature of a vow: whenever I had some reason to cry, I would each time cry myself out and, after the tears were over, I would have a small break and then shed some extra, additional tears in memory of the squirrel that had been tormented to death. In this way I would prove to the adults that I had not forgotten that feeling of injury and sorrow, let them realize every time what bad, malicious and cruel people they were. But I have already remarked somewhere else that my two chief failings are being too trustful and too forgiving; and that is what has happened: not a trace of all that terrible bitterness and burning fury has remained in my soul, although I can still see plainly, as if it were here before me now, that little bloody face in the chink beneath the cross-beam.

The second incident, which has proved just as impossible to forget, is, perhaps, even more terrible than the first.

Setting off on a walk, I noticed a group of lads – Shurka Ulitin, Kolka Grubov and Borka Moskovkin, all of them older than I – conferring together mysteriously in the grounds of the church near the church porch. Well, it is quite usual for younger children to hover around older lads and even youths. It is as if they do not notice them and everyone carries on just as if they were not there. That was exactly what happened on this occasion – none of the older boys paid any attention to me at all.

'Right then,' Shurka Ulitin was saying – he was evidently the senior one present, the leader or, let us say, organizer – 'we'll use three sticks. I reckon that will do it.'

I saw that each of the three boys did indeed have a good hazel stick in his hand.

'Right. . . . Three sticks it is . . . ' said Borka Moskovkin in support of the leader.

'Perhaps we could give a stick to him too?' Shurka Ulitin nodded in my direction.

'He would only get in the way. We'll manage on our own.'

'Let's go, then.'

And off they went into the corner of the church grounds, an area overgrown with nettles, motherwort and mournful burdocks. Naturally I strung along after them. Amidst the high, burgeoning grass the lads had made a businesslike job of trampling the grass underfoot to create a small, flat space. I still could not understand what they had in mind, otherwise there would have been time to run away or at least screw up my eyes.

'Let's have it,' commanded Shurka.

Then Borka Moskovkin took out from inside his coat a tiny (but not so tiny that it did not know what was going on) little white kitten with one black ear, a pink nose and bright eyes. Doubtless it had other black spots on it too, on its back or sides, but now I recall only its white fur, pink nose, bright eyes and, finally, that little black ear.

I should mention that I spent all my childhood with kittens, I played with them with bows on pieces of string, they slept under my blanket and to this day I cannot name a more delightful creature than a kitten.

Borka Moskovkin took the white kitten out from under his coat and put it on the ground. The kitten was frightened after the dark and lay close to the ground, looking round all the time. Immediately, just as had been agreed, the three sticks came down – Boom! Boom! Boom! – on top of that living, enchanting, helpless creature. Their blows seemed somehow muffled. Once again I saw blood coming from a little pink nose as another tiny body lay stretched out in ever-weakening convulsions. . . .

Lord, why did you show me that?

13

SOME TIME AGO THERE APPEARED IN OUR VILLAGE A LITTLE
word which until then had never before been heard there
(and the village is mentioned in documents dating from
the twelfth century), a word which indeed had never been
heard in Russia at all: 'authorized'. I heard about it right
away because those who were authorized would put up in
our house. Perhaps that was only fair because with two
storeys, it was the roomiest house in the village. At one
time – and that 'one time' had been just a few years
previously or, if not a few, then no more than ten – there
had been an elder in the village and *desyatskies*:[23] these
were the oldest inhabitants in each group of ten village
houses. So then, if a traveller or wanderer of some sort,
or a late passer-by, on foot or otherwise, found himself
caught out in bad weather, he would certainly not be left
without a place to spend the night. The elder and the
desyatskies knew whose turn it was to take someone in for
the night and would lead him straight to the appropriate
house. Objections were out of the question: it is your turn
and that is the end of it, yours today and your neighbour's
tomorrow.

Later on, however, in place of the elder and the
desyatskies there appeared something called the 'Selkoko'.
None of the peasants, of course, knew what it was or how
to make sense of the name, just as even now I am not
absolutely clear whether it stood for the Rural Committee
of Communists or the Rural Peasant Committee. All I
remember is that Pavel Ivanovich Ulitin was made chairman

of the Selkoko (I cannot imagine why – he was just an ordinary peasant like any other). Incidentally, he was the father of Shurka, the ringleader during the slaughter of the kitten.

Doubtless it was the Selkoko which gave the order: the authorized officials were to be sent to our house. Perhaps, though, the rural Soviet was already in existence by then, or rather it surely did exist by that time, and possibly it was already in charge of everything, both in Alepino itself and in the surrounding fifteen smaller villages, whereas the Selkoko (if it was indeed the Rural Committee of Communists) was in charge of the rural Soviet, or someone ran the rural Soviet from on high by means of this, as they would say, administrative cell, the Selkoko. Or someone up above ran the peasants' lives with the aid of both the rural Soviet and the Selkoko.

Authorized officials came and went in our house, I do not remember them all, and now in retrospect I cannot even say – cannot, so to speak, figure it out these days – why they came at all, until the time when collectivization was announced. However, I do recall one of them, one indeed of those who predated the collective farms; perhaps he was the very last one before they were established. He liked to play with me or, I should say, to tease me, often reducing me to tears. I remember him first and foremost because he once held me up in the palm of his outstretched hand and exclaimed in surprise: 'Well now, mate, you're more than a pood!' (So, again, you can see how old I was then.) He also teased me by coming up to me in a businesslike manner with a rope and saying he was about to tie me up and take me away somewhere. I can even remember his surname – Egorov.

I should say that I felt in my infant's heart what I suppose must have been an instinctive dislike for all these authorized people. I felt they were my enemies, and it is possible that they in turn looked upon me as some sort of little wolf as my eyes flashed at them from the corner. (Incidentally, that was one of the childhood nicknames that my sister Katyusha bestowed upon me. Sometimes she would call me 'white cabbage' on account of my head with its high crown and the tuft of hair over the right side of my forehead, and sometimes, as I said, little wolf. Let me mention in passing that I wrote the poem 'Wolves' almost forty years later.) And so, then, the authorized official, Egorov, liked to tease me.

Perhaps I used to run away and hide whenever this happened, I do not know and cannot remember. But once, driven into a corner, I suddenly hurled myself at Egorov and, thumping him with my little four-year-old (or less?) fists, howled and shrieked 'I'll kill you, I really will, I'll kill you!' This, I have no doubt, amused everyone greatly. Yet now a thought occurs to me that saddens me: could it be that those seconds were the only time in my life when I was completely and utterly sincere? After that the years, the decades of compliance and loyalty set in, years, to use more convoluted language, of collaborationism and conformism.

I recall two other such authorized officials even more vividly. Their stay in our house turned out to be, as philosophers and theologians say these days, providential. Apart from that, I had grown up a little by the time in question. I have already written about these two people in my long work, A Drop of Dew, but that description of them naturally contained its share of loyalty and conformism. Everything there was wrapped up in cotton wool so as to be suitable for publication in the journal Znamia,[24] and then as a separate book.

At the moment I do not have by me, here in Karacharovo where these lines are being written, a copy of A Drop of Dew, and so I cannot check what I wrote there about this episode. Perhaps I shall repeat myself in some respects, but in others I know for sure that I shall not. The names of these people were Irinin and Losev and they were sent to our village with the uncompromising task of organizing collective farms in the village and in all the surrounding fifteen hamlets.

Those who were there, somewhere up above (and the plans had come to maturity as early as 1921 at the 9th Congress of the RCP (B)[25] when Trotsky and Lenin were still in power), well knew what it was they were about to do and why they were about to do it. The free and resourceful Russian peasantry had to be turned into a faceless army of landless, obedient and, most importantly, virtually unpaid slaves. The task was to scoop all the resources out of Russia, out of the Russian land, for the sake of some mythical world revolution (or, possibly, a simpler explanation was that those who did it wanted to be in a position to use the might of the state and military in order to cling to power themselves). Quite recently, to digress for a moment, in the offices of the Central Committee in Tashkent, an important figure in the hierarchy of the Uzbek SSR[26] honoured me with a conversation. He said, as if boasting: 'Every year we send off to you people in Moscow seven million karakul lamb pelts.'

'What do you mean, "to you people"?' I was truly surprised. 'I have personally never seen a single karakul pelt in my life. Where do they get to?'

'They contribute to the might of the state,' answered the man from the Central Committee.

I might have been forgiven for asking: who needs this 'might of the state' and why?

They need it in order to preserve this systematized siphoning off of resources.

I should imagine that they do at least pay something to the Uzbeks, as well as to the Tadjiks, Kirghiz, Turkmens and Kazakhs (how many million pelts does that add up to?) for the pelts; they give them at least a few symbolic roubles, just as they pay for their cotton (a raw material of strategic importance!), whereas for decades the Russian peasants were paid nothing for their wheat, rye, peas, buckwheat, potatoes, beetroot (from the Ukraine), flax (from Vologda), milk and meat. Everything that the collective-farm workers produced was taken by the state for virtually nothing, and for every so-called workday they paid out in some places from three to five copecks. No one worked more than four hundred workdays a year. Four hundred multiplied by five (by fifty before the monetary reform) gives us twenty roubles a year. Well, even if we say two hundred in pre-reform money, it was still only what a town-dweller earned in a month. (And on top of that, various taxes had to be paid out of it.)

In those same days, somewhere at the start of the twenties, it was decided that: 'In order to drive the Russian peasantry, and all the other nations in the country, into collective farms – that is, turn them into those unpaid armies of labourers – 10 per cent of the peasants have to be physically annihilated. Then the other 90 per cent will be ready to form themselves into collective farms.' I do not know in whose criminal head this figure first arose, but it became a reality and when in 1929 the mechanism of collectivization was started up, it was based specifically on that figure. Remember that 10 per cent of the peasantry of those days was six million families. I do not know how many people that meant, given the large number of children in each family. A figure exists, one which admittedly is difficult to check, to the effect that about fifteen million totally innocent peasants perished during the period.

They took them off in sledges through the snowstorms and biting winter frosts to the nearest railway station. There they packed them into unheated goods wagons and transported them for days at a time into the north or to Siberia. Those who survived these deportations were kept until the spring in former monasteries, where they died like flies. In the spring (I was told about what happened on the Ob), as soon as the ice had gone, they filled unheated barges with them and 'let them go' down the Ob, and after that they took them into the taiga via the Sosva and Vasyugan, tributaries of the Ob. Here they were set ashore in the mosquito-infested taiga, where they were at the mercy of fate. Out of every five hundred people, two or three survived. And there was also this further

125

subtlety. The men who were capable of working were immediately sorted out and dispatched to the White Sea–Baltic Canal; only the women, children and old men were taken off to Siberia. One such old man told my friend, Zhenya Maltsev, that, after he (a carpenter) had been set ashore in the taiga along with the others (they left them two axes and a sack of flour), he had personally put up five hundred crosses over the peasants' graves – the graves of holy martyrs, men and women alike.

I keep meaning to write about how the well-known Mansi poet, Yuvan Shestalov (the Mansi used to be called the Vogul), took me to his homeland, to the small town of Berezov, and on through the taiga along the River Sosva to his native village or, more accurately, settlement. There was a great deal that I found absorbing at the time (I really shall write about it!), but one particular detail must be mentioned immediately. I asked if the settlement had been in existence for a long time. There were even trees in front of some of the houses, bird-cherries, but the houses were somehow strange, almost like barracks, as if there were a number of families to each house.

'Well, the settlement was created by special category deportees.'

'What sort of "special category deportees"?'

'Former kulaks. From the Ukraine. They brought them here and set them ashore in the wilds of the taiga. They would come up to our nomad encampments and tents, dying of hunger. Well, sometimes our people would give them something to eat. Those who survived built themselves houses here . . . '

'And what happened after that?'

'After that, when we were struck by famine, it was our turn to go to them. They, the ones who had survived, were sowing potatoes by that time and even growing rye. So now it was they who fed us.'

What an idyll!

So then, the names of the authorized officials in our village were Irinin and Losev. Irinin had one arm missing (from the Civil War?); he was tall and lean and his face was somehow bumpy and very harsh-looking, its redness enhanced by a grey crewcut. Losev, on the other hand, was undersized, with a round face and dark-brown hair. Irinin was entirely engrossed in the idea, in the task the Party had set him, and was ready at any moment to destroy anything he had to or kill if it came to it, but Losev was sociable, good fun, and he liked to play the violin. In the evenings he would visit our sexton and church reader, Nikolay Alekseevich Nadezhdin (it is terrible to think of the authorized officials of the time), and they would play duets together. The sexton and church reader also had a violin, evidently. Anyhow, not many free evenings came the officials' way. It was specifically in the evenings, up until midnight, that they held meetings in the school, attempting by means of persuasion and deceitful promises of a blissful life, as well as with threats, to drive all the peasants into the collective farm. I remember all this from mere snatches of conversation. One day half the village would put their names down for the collective farm and the next day the same people would come with written declarations to the effect that they were leaving it (having had second thoughts overnight). None of them knew that they were all doomed already to collective-farm life and that they were simply caught up in a game of cat and mouse.

As for the dispossession of the kulaks and their deportation to distant parts, that is, the class struggle at village level, all of that passed somehow unnoticed in our area. The main point is that the collectivization process itself for some reason took place in the region around Moscow a whole year later than in areas distant from the centre, when the principal wave of violence and destruction, the major impact of the 'great break' (of the peasants' backbone), had already subsided. Possibly, also, the article 'Dizzy with Success' had already appeared in print (a favourite trick: do what you must and then blame it all on others).[27]

In any event the lot of dispossession as kulaks fell upon only two of our peasant households: the Grubovs in the hamlet of Ostanikha and, alas, us in our village.

Aleksey Pavlovich Grubov was a slaughterer – that is, a specialist in the slaughtering of livestock: cows, a bull if necessary, sheep, piglets. His speciality was almost as indispensable as that of stove-maker, saddler, carpenter, tawer and so on. Well, it was the done thing to reward the slaughterer in some way for his efforts, usually in kind, and for that reason the Grubovs lived a little better, a little more prosperously than others. So the decision was taken to dispossess them. However, they were down to half-measures by that stage: an inventory was to be made of their property, which would be auctioned off, but the family was not to be exiled. Of that entire chain of events a single, tragicomic episode impressed itself upon my memory. Auntie Nyusha Grubova, a beautiful and, at that time, still young mother of three lads, seized hold of her feather bed and would not give it up. Her reason for doing this brought some amusement to the crowd of gapers: 'I lost my virginity in it and won't let it go!'

But, of course, they took the feather bed away from her in the end and one of the neighbours (yes, a neighbour, and here you can see an example of the total betrayal of one friend by another) bought it for next to nothing. And what if they had all refused to buy it? What would the authorized officials have done with a feather bed? Take it back to their regional office? What would they have done with the rest of the goods and chattels in the inventory? But no, those same Ostanikha folk, neighbours and even distant relatives, bought everything up and carried it off to their homes. (The Grubovs themselves after this event left Ostanikha and settled in our village. All three boys – Kolka, Valka and Borka – were my sort of age, we went about and played together as infants and later, when we were older, we attended school together. None of them returned from the war. More detailed information about them can be found, again, in *A Drop of Dew*.)

In our case it was decided to act with greater cruelty: the property was to be listed and sold off and the people themselves exiled and taken away to torture and death; but at this point, as I understood it, or, to be more exact, as I understand it now, a heated argument over us broke out between Irinin and Losev. Irinin favoured evicting our family, but Losev was for leaving us in the house as we were.

They went off somewhere outside the village, into the wintry haze of a light snowstorm, in order to argue over our fate and disappeared in the forest for about two hours. I spent the time sitting, dressed in three coats, one on top of another. Someone had told Mother that they would not allow us to take any clothes with us, although they would not remove anything that was already on us. (Does anyone want me to forgive and forget that?) When they returned – remember, they were billeted in our house – Losev was excited and in good spirits, but Irinin was imperviously sombre, so that it was impossible to tell immediately how our fate had been decided. I do not recall this myself, but my mother maintained afterwards that Irinin suddenly held out a peppermint cake for me and at that moment it was clear that we were saved. On a number of occasions in the course of her life Mother made sure I understood: 'Remember, it was Losev who saved us. I constantly pray to God for him, and you, even if you don't pray, you must still remember that it was Losev who saved us.'

When later in *A Drop of Dew* I came to describe this episode, surrounding it with padding and couching it in gentle, rosy hues, both of them, Irinin and Losev, unexpectedly responded and sent me letters. Irinin asked me to see what I could do to get his pension raised and Losev sent me a warm invitation to come fishing: he was working as a livestock specialist on a state farm somewhere in the vicinity of Astrakhan. For a few years running I kept meaning to visit him with, as they say, the most serious intentions in mind. We corresponded, during which time he retired and moved from the state farm to Astrakhan itself. I meant to visit him there too, and we corresponded again; but, there we are, I have still not been to this day (a typical example of our Russian swinishness).

So then, they carried some pieces of furniture out of the house and auctioned them off, which left us with only the 'downstairs' – that is, the bottom floor of the house. Upstairs, in the room where I had been born – the so-called 'middle room' – the office of the newly formed state farm was accommodated. The big room at the front was turned into a club. All I remember of the time the office was in our house are the thick clouds of tobacco smoke which must have made it impossible not only to breathe, but even to see, your eyes smarted so much. The house, however, was not very suited for use as an office and they soon moved to another place, into a house that had been brought from another village. But the club stayed in our house for a long time and, since the young people entertained themselves exclusively with dancing, we found ourselves living down below with the whole house shaking around us grotesquely until long after midnight. Later, when I grew up, I took part in these evening festivities myself. I also remember the bewilderment with which my sleepy, dishevelled father (now old and decrepit) would come 'up top' late at night and watch as a herd of young people whirled, yelled folk rhymes and stamped in his house. They weakened the whole house to such an extent that they had to look for other accommodation whether they liked it or not. The club moved into the former fire-engine shed, so my old people lived out their final years peacefully and quietly, albeit in a rickety house. When I went home for the holidays, I would use the whole of the top storey, where I would read or write by the light of a paraffin lamp, as I still had to in those days. By 1960 (my father had died by then) it had become virtually impossible to live in the house and I undertook major repairs. Of course everything had to be changed inside the house, but its external appearance remained (and remains) exactly as it had been originally.

It is left for me to describe now how Stepanida Ivanovna would repeatedly go off somewhere, some district or regional office, and I think she even visited Mikhail Ivanovich Kalinin.[28] This was called 'taking steps'. She went on busying herself with these 'steps' until she finally achieved the full official rehabilitation of our family after our dispossession as kulaks. It was decided that we had the right to reclaim everything that had been taken from the house and sold (as well as the house itself, its upper storey). This was perfectly possible to do: we knew of course who had bought what at the auction, we knew where our sideboard was, where the bed and wardrobe (clothes cupboard) were and so on; but we did not bother to take anything back (although the decision was that we could reclaim everything without paying, not that we should buy it all back). The only exception was the cow.

I shall never ever forget that quiet, warm, gentle, yet autumnal (October, most likely) day, when Mother and I went to the hamlet of Volkovo (six to seven kilometres from our village) for the cow. I could not have been more than six, and in all probability that was the first time I had made such a long journey on foot. It was after all twelve to fourteen kilometres there and back. We walked along quietly and unhurriedly, keeping to the winding river, although, rather than go along the river-bank as such, we stayed a little way off, following scarcely visible paths from meadow to meadow, hill to hill and wood to wood. Not many people, of course, ever needed to walk on foot from our village to Volkovo. I remember it was warm, although the birches were already littering the green grass with their little yellow leaves; I remember how we rested under a fir which stood alone on the slope of a hill, and I remember the feeling of peace in the world and in my soul. That was because we were making the journey not to give our cow away or sell her, but to bring her back.

We led the cow home on a rope and walked even more slowly. When we stopped for a rest we left the cow free to graze and she would nibble at the grass without straying far, so that the journey took us a whole day. That quiet, warm, peaceful autumn day is even more precious to me because at no other time in my life, neither I think before nor since, did I have the chance to spend a whole day alone with my mother. Increasingly I would have her company only at odd moments: she would give me something to eat, put me to bed, make me pray, call me home if I stayed out too long playing or sit by me when I was ill, and all that would be mixed up with the rest of the domestic hustle and bustle. But for the whole of that day it was just the two of us. There we are, wending our unhurried way, it is a quiet, warm day and we are taking our cow back home. Perhaps there never was a happier day in my life.

14

THIS SHORT CHAPTER SHOULD, STRICTLY SPEAKING, BE placed in the second part of the book[29] because both events described happened during my schooldays, whereas my idea was to finish the first part with my arrival at school. However, the time in question also relates to my very early childhood and it is still not certain whether I shall manage (for many reasons) to write the second part. Also, the memories involved are bright and fresh and, what is more, they serve in their own way to sketch in the setting and atmosphere, so to speak, of the time. You might even say that they have, as far as they go, social significance, although I shall be speaking about the only two drubbings that I caused my self-controlled and kindhearted parents to give me throughout my childhood.

Suddenly, as if the world were about to end or the plague were upon us, our village was gripped by a passion for gambling, a passion that reached epidemic proportions. People, young and old, would spend the long winter evenings playing lotto. They would gather together in a number of peasant houses, where so many people would be sitting round the table that at times it was a real crush. The old women, who were not up to playing by the 'move-along' method, would have handfuls of buttons, coppers and little cardboard squares in order to 'block out' any numbers that coincided with the figures which were being called out. The younger people quickly mastered the progressive 'move-along' method and all they needed were three buttons or coins for each card, corresponding to the quantity of lines of numbers on it. If a number came up, the button would be moved along one square (on to an empty one), and it would soon be at the edge of the card. 'One at a time,' the player shouts. That meant that he needed only one number to win and the counters had to be taken out of the bag no longer in handfuls but strictly one at a time. There was a point in this because of course the caller could look across and see what number was needed to win and, with a handful of counters in his hand, he could take his time and not shout out the required number. He might even play clever and imperceptibly put the counter that the player needed and was waiting for back into the bag; but no, as soon as someone shouted 'One at a time' they would begin to take the counters out of the bag one at a time. Each counter was given a nickname: 90 (the highest counter) was Grandfather; 80, Grandmother; 77, hatchets (or Semen Semenych); 22, ducks; 11, drumsticks. . . . I do not remember the others, but there were some clever callers who shouted out virtually all the figures by their nicknames.

Well . . . you cannot lose much at lotto. The stake, as I recall, was two copecks a card. It was somehow not the done thing for the grown lads to waste their energy on lotto cards along with the old and very young, and so they got together on their own and played furiously at pontoon, or 'twenty-one', where the money involved was different, as was the sense of excitement. However, we young lotto-players very quickly discovered for ourselves a faster and, you could say, more radical way of playing. We would stake, let us say, five copecks apiece. Then each of us in turn would delve into the bag of lotto counters and pull one out. Whoever had the 'bigger' counter would take the stake. The whole process took just a few seconds. You might agree to stake five copecks each, but then again, it might be ten copecks, or it could be more. Then one day I lost all my money playing this game.

The excitement of gambling had already taken us all over, I simply had to play the next day – what was I to do? So,

I slipped my hand into Father's purse (a black leather purse with two little metal balls at a slight angle instead of a lock, a classical Russian purse) and took out a few copeck coins from it: two twenties, two fifteens and a few tens.

I probably made a number of repeat runs and it was soon noticed. Father did not keep such a huge quantity of money in his purse that he did not at once become aware when it began to diminish. Most likely, even though he noticed it immediately, he waited a little in order to see what would happen next, and when he was sure that things were exactly as he suspected and that his small son was nothing but a petty thief, he had a word with Stepanida Ivanovna. They evidently decided at this family council that Mother should be the one to punish me.

I have to say at this point that children were never beaten in our family. Things never went beyond clips behind the ear or slaps. If anyone slipped up, Father would lift his heavy, rough, calloused hand – a hand used to ploughing and mowing – and deliver a light blow to the back of one's head. That was as far as the punishment went. If Mother had to do the same thing, she would bring her hand down somewhere soft, a slap rather than a clip. A funny thing happened once. My sister (and godmother) Valentina shouted at me for some reason: 'You'll get a white slap now'. She said 'white', I suppose, meaning the slap would land somewhere soft and bare. I could not have understood the word 'slap' at the time and I imagined something white like cottage cheese, good tasting, or something cooked that happened to be white, like a pancake or a flapjack. After that, to the amusement of everyone in the house, I spent half a day pestering Valentina, asking her over and over again: 'Let me have a white slap, go on, let me have a white slap.'

And so they decided to give me a proper thrashing. Mother was entrusted with this task, which was a greater punishment for her than it was for me. Not long before she died – that is, about thirty-five years after the event – she kept on trying to ask my forgiveness for something and I could not understand for what, and it was only later, after she had gone, that it suddenly came to me with a shock: of course, she was asking forgiveness for the thrashing, for that act of bodily chastisement.

Mother first warned me that she was going to beat me, told me why and then beat me with a twisted-up towel. She beat me and wept at the same time. She cried more than I did. I remember that it was not at all painful (what is a twisted-up towel – hardly a stick, a whip, or a strap), but the process itself was such a torment to us both that I still remember the whole experience down to the last detail and, as it turned out, that day weighed upon Stepanida Ivanovna right until she died.

On the surface, the second event looked trifling compared with the first (which had involved, after all, stealing from Father's purse, and that was a moral problem as well as being the first appearance of a character trait which might, possibly, have had far-reaching consequences, and anyway it was a terrible thing to do, if not a crime), but the second event, the second event was exactly that, a chance event but, with the way things were in those days, it could have led to a tragedy of huge proportions and must have given Father a real fright.

Earlier in these sketches, in the appropriate place, I described how a great many different objects would find their way in amongst the old honeycombs that Father would bring back from various places in bast sacks and cloth bags as raw material for making wax. Most often they contained small change, coins, but other things would crop up, too: a brass window bolt, a nail, a screw, a brass door-handle, hinge-plates for a door or window-frame, a small penknife. . . . Once, however, a real loaded revolver turned up. It was a very old revolver with an ancient mechanism (if I were to thumb through an album containing pictures of weapons I should be sure to recognize it). I remember that it had a cylinder from which small brass pins protruded opposite each chamber, so that they would be struck by the trigger, and that bullets were visible in

136

the chambers of the cylinder. And it is a matter of amazement, considering that we treated this object the way boys would, endlessly clicking away with it, that not a single shot occurred. My father evidently forgot about this find after some time, or considered it lost, whereas in actual fact I had it. It was well hidden in the attic, but from time to time I would take it from its secret hiding-place and run off with the other lads to the 'precipice' (a wooden sandy slope overlooking the river), in order to play at being Chapaev or someone like that. I have forgotten who we pretended to be and what games we played.

Nor do I remember why or in what circumstances the boys and I needed the revolver on that fateful day. It would be more correct to write 'were going to need it', because I had removed it from its hiding-place and, without taking it all the way to school, had hidden it again, this time in the church grounds near an old lime, in amongst the dry leaves left from the previous autumn. When our lessons were over and we came back to this place, the revolver was missing.

Afterwards it was established that a certain lad – Vitka Moskovkin, actually – had looked through his window and seen me hiding something in the church grounds near the old lime and decided to find out, after I had gone, what precisely it was that I had hidden. The rest goes without saying. . . .

The rumour that we were keeping, or at least had been keeping until then, a revolver in our house, needed no help in being spread throughout the village. Remember, this happened right at the beginning of the thirties. People were being picked up, deported and annihilated for lesser misdemeanours than that (and for no misdemeanours at all). You can understand how frightened Father was. This was no occasion for delegating my punishment to Stepanida Ivanovna. But she was there all the time, she cried and wept and put her hands under Father's strap to protect me, and under his palms when he was slapping my cheeks and temples before returning to the strap. That happened fifty years ago, but it seems like only yesterday.

15

IN OUR VILLAGE THERE WAS NO HIGHER TRIGONOMETRICAL point than the 'little cross'. That was what they would say if they had to say something was high: 'higher than the little cross'. When they said this they meant not the cross on the church, but the one on the bell-tower. In Russia the crosses on the bell-towers, at least in the rural areas (in the towns I think the opposite sometimes happened), were always higher than those on the church.

Nor was there a higher point in the village (or in the surrounding area) from which to survey everything around than the bell-tower. Here I mean not the cross, which was way out of reach, but the platform in the bell-tower where the bells hung and which had wide openings to all four sides, so that the sound of the bells in the morning and evening might waft freely away into the distance, over the fields, forests and meadows, until it reached other bell-towers like the one it had left. The chiming of the bells at Easter and the slow strokes of the large bell at funerals, a sound like the march of fate, would drift away unhindered from the bell-tower in all directions, floating over the earth to fade in the summer-green (or frosty, snow-covered) distance.

You could not see many other bell-towers from our village, even if you looked from the bell-tower: there was one in Cherkutino, four kilometres away, one in Spasskoe (which peeped out from behind the dark mass of a pine forest), that was five or six kilometres from us, and another one in Eltesunovo, also the other side of a forest some seven kilometres away. I no longer recall whether the bell-tower in the village of Rozhdestveno could be seen in the far distance. It was very high and should have been visible but, on the other hand, it was at least nine kilometres away. Those were all the bell-towers that could be seen in those days from our Alepino vantage-point. Yet in the village of Vasilevo, three kilometres from us, beyond the kitchen gardens, there was, as people would say now, an observation platform from which twenty-one sugary-white bell-towers could be counted in the blue-green distance of the Koloksha valley and in the hills beyond the Koloksha. What is more, in the area of Shakhmatovo made famous by Blok,[30] in the hills above the River Lutosnya, there was another such platform from which more than ten bell-towers could be counted. Now imagine them all starting to ring at the same time. . . .

As is known, the Government recently had a moment of generosity and gave the former Danilov Monastery to the Patriarchate, to do with it as it saw fit. I should say the ruins, the broken remains of the former Danilov Monastery. In the thirties they used to tip earth there whilst building the Metro, then it became a prison and was occupied by a colony of under-age criminals. In the end only ruins remained of the monastery. And so these ruins were given to the Patriarchate, along with permission to restore the monastery or, more accurately, to build it anew. I visited the building site when work was in full swing. There was a real buzz of activity and the building was advancing at such a pace that in the course of a year they built more than the state could have done in fifteen years. Somewhere in the depths of Yaroslavl Region, in a village in a forest they found (miracle of miracles) the only bells, in all probability, that had not been dashed to the ground throughout the whole territory of the USSR, with the exception of Rostov Veliky and the Kremlin. I am sure that it must have been the only such village in the whole of the USSR. These bells (which would anyway have tumbled down soon, taking the bell-tower with them) were brought to the Danilov Monastery and hoisted up into the newly rebuilt bell-tower. However, I saw them when they were still standing on the ground. I read on the big one that it weighed two hundred and ten poods. That surprised me, which is why I remembered about it now. Only two hundred and ten poods for such a colossal bell! Of course I well recall the inscription on our bell in Alepino, which proclaimed that it weighed two hundred and seventy poods, fourteen pounds. There was also an inscription in Slavonic ornamental script to the effect that it had been presented by the peasant Mikhail Dmitrievich Soloukhin – that is, my grandfather's brother. Nowadays I doubt if the entire region, never mind the local district, would be up to casting a bell such as that peasant was able to make. Two hundred and seventy poods. The proportion of silver in the bell was also indicated on it, but I have forgotten the figure.

Admittedly the peasants of Cherkutino outshone those of Alepino (it was the thing in those days to try to outdo the neighbouring villages by having a higher bell-tower or bigger bells) when they cast a monster weighing five hundred poods. But a crack appeared in it during the casting process, they did not bother to recast it and for that reason it produced a defective, jingling sound. It was no match for the magnificent, full-bodied, silvery bronze sound of our bell.

There were different categories of bells. The big one was called simply that, 'the Big Bell'. They rang it during church services, weddings and funerals. Ordinarily no one would dare set its massive, forged iron clapper (the thick end of which was the size of a horse's head) in motion to produce its staggering sound. That would happen only if there were some great calamity; and I think the Big Bell was allowed to be struck if a fire broke out in the village itself. For all other occasions there was a tocsin – a bell weighing twenty-nine poods.

They rang the tocsin with rapid strokes (this was referred to as striking or beating the tocsin) and, in all truth, I have never since met, despite hearing a good many different sirens and bells during ground-attack alerts, a more disturbing or, I should say, ominous signal than the ringing of our tocsin.

Apart from that there was a chime of bells, each one smaller than the other, so that they probably weighed from five down to one pood. There were eight of them hanging on a single cross-beam in the northern aperture of the bell-tower. They were each attached to strings which the ringer fixed to the fingers of both hands by means of loops, and he made the bells chime by pulling on these strings. The tocsin also added to the chiming of these bells. The string that was attached to it nearly reached the floor and a board was inserted into a loop at the bottom. The bell-ringer would place his foot on this board at the right moment and make the tocsin ring. At the same time a different ringer would be thumping on the Big Bell.

All these bells together made up a remarkable musical instrument, or rather an orchestra; but the music was designed to be listened to at some distance. After all, even a shepherd's horn of the type played in the Vladimir district, when heard close at hand, seems too loud, like a strident squeal, whereas from a distance, from the other side of a field, a ravine, a river, a meadow or a wood, especially in the misty dawn, can there be anything more wonderful, purer or sweeter? One Easter morning, when I was probably about four or five, Father took me with him up into the bell-tower in order to show me how the bells were rung. As I watched two young men, I no longer recall who, began to swing the clapper on the Big Bell and, when it hit the edge of the bell for the first time, I was deafened, astounded and frightened. I began to cry and had to be briskly removed from the bell-tower. Indeed, the sound of the Big Bell close to could be compared, most probably, to that of a cannon being fired right next to you.

. . . They deceived the people shamelessly and brazenly, like little children, when they told them that the country needed non-ferrous metal to make guns. There was a convenient historical precedent to cite, in that Peter had also turned bells into guns during the war with Sweden.[31] But, in the first place, not all of them, not all the bells from the whole of Russia were used; secondly, they recast them and hung them again at the end of the war; thirdly, modern guns were made of steel, not bronze; fourthly, Russia (before the Bolsheviks) always maintained her weapons to modern standards and had no need to cast down any bells; fifthly, I personally saw, about ten years later, a whole mound of broken bells at the railway station in Undol – the point being that they smashed the bells up there and then in the villages and took them away in pieces. In other words, there was no particular need for non-ferrous metal, if in ten years they had not bothered to take the pieces away to be melted down, preferring to leave them lying around the station. The important thing had been to cast them down and smash them. The important thing had been to humiliate the people. The important thing had been to break their spirit once again, this time with the bells. The first time their spirit had been broken was during the collectivization and the formation of the collective farms, and this was done by taking away their land and their horses, their initiative and their sense of being masters on their own land. 'The year of the great break': it was the backbone of the Russian peasants and people that was broken. Just as, when an individual person stands up manfully to something, trying to resist and hold his own, it is enough to break him once (interrogators would say 'crack'), so it is with an entire people. Break them once and then do what you like with them. In order to reinforce the first break – brought about by collectivization – it was decided to humiliate the people and break them again by casting the bells down throughout the length and breadth of Russia, by robbing the country and the people of sound, of their tongue, and by plunging them into deafness and dumbness. If they, the people, had nothing to say even about that, you really could go ahead

142

and do with them what you wanted and mould them into any shape you liked.

At that time I was already going to school; it was my first or second year – most likely my first. That means I was seven years old and therefore this all took place in 1931; but possibly it was the following year. The Big Bell thumped to the ground whilst we, village children, were all at our lessons. It happened in our absence; and indeed, of the whole business of casting down the bells, only a few episodes have remained in my memory. First, there is the crowd of women in front of the entrance to the bell-tower. Some strange men with ropes are standing before them. The women have barred the entrance and are not allowing the strangers through, they are chattering loudly whilst the strangers, those who were to do the casting down, the bells' executioners, are trying to force their way through the crowd and get into the bell-tower.

Try as they might, they did not manage to do this. A peculiar kind of battle went on all day, then perhaps understanding that they were no match for the crowd of women, or perhaps that they had lost their chance for that day, the bell-wreckers retreated. Of all the women who were shouting and blocking the way to the bell-tower I remember Shurka Baklanikhina best. She was evidently their leader, organizer, inspirer and chief. Incidentally to this day (she is now of course a very elderly lady), whenever I meet her, I involuntarily greet her with a little extra respect and esteem on account of the 'day of the bells'.

The second episode I remember is when the entire population of Alepino was assembled together in a crowd which this time included all the menfolk and, as will be apparent, the children. There we were, standing in the church grounds before the church, whilst a speech was being delivered by the chairman of the rural Soviet, Alexander Nikolaevich Nikolaypetrov, who was actually a Soloukhin (just as, by the way, Shurka Baklanikhina is also officially a Soloukhin; almost everyone in our village is a Soloukhin, that is why they have second surnames

143

and are known 'for village purposes' as Baklanikhins, Simionovs, Moskovkins and even, as you see, Nikolay-petrovs). In the intense manner that you find at public meetings, he was shouting something at the Alepino folk and they were listening in silence. In fact he was trying to win them over and persuade them of the need to throw the bells down. From all his jabbering I remember but one single argument: 'Imagine a war starting. The enemy has three guns, but we have only two. The enemy will defeat us. We also must have three guns, if not four.' That was the sort of logic the powers that be used when talking with the people in those days.

This speech was not enough. The women who had taken part in the earlier battle were called one by one into the rural Soviet and each told something there individually. The next day but one, when the bells' executioners approached the entrance to the bell-tower, no one stood in their way any more.

It was early morning. I had not yet left for school. I remember my mother looking out of the window at the bell-tower. One of the 'skilled workers' brushed the dust off from a cross-beam with his mitten and at that point Mother burst into tears and began to wail: 'They're brushing the dust off . . . they're brushing the dust off. . . .' I do not recall any more and, most likely, I did not see any more. When they actually threw the bells down we children were sitting in school at our lessons, and quite possibly the schoolmistress was reading us verses by Zharov or Bezymensky.[32]

16

SO THEN, IT IS 1931. I AM SEVEN. IN THE VILLAGE AND surrounding hamlets the collective farm has been established – that is, the peasants have been condemned to joyless, forced, almost unpaid labour, labour performed to a signal, at the ring of a bell (to which end they left one small bell from the chime, about a pood and a half in weight, which they hung on a post). 1931. Throughout the land the bells have been cast down from the bell-towers. In place of the ancient village names in our area – Prokoshikha, Brod, Ostanikha, Kuryanikha, Venki, Pugovtsino, Vishenki, Lutino, Krivets, Zelniki, Rozh-destveno, Ratmirovo, Spasskoe, Snegirevo, Ratislovo – in place of these ancient, centuries-old Russian names, each with its own history, in every document and speech, in the regional newspaper and district rag, in news-sheets on walls and in all those miserable charts and graphs other names started to appear: 'Red Communist Avant-garde', 'The Road to Socialism', 'Pace-setter', 'Forward', 'Red Profintern', 'Champion', 'Rosa Luxemburg', 'Red Banner', 'Lenin's', 'May Day'. . . .

Our village looked at first as though it was going to be lucky. They called the collective farm in the village 'Culturist' – also nothing to write home about, but still, not 'Red Profintern'; but this name turned out to be temporary. When they began amalgamating the collective farms, at one time we were called '40 Years of October', then for a while we were the 'Khrushchev Collective Farm' and now we come under the 'Lenin Collective Farm'. The hamlets are disintegrating and shrinking (sometimes they disappear completely from the face of the earth). They are gathered together twenty or thirty at a time and turned into collective farms. I have already had occasion to write (in the story 'Trouble with Pigeons') that the school in our village has long been closed – there were no children left to teach. The whole area had produced three pupils, whereas in 1931, as our former schoolmistress told me later, in the four classes of our Alepino primary school there were one hundred and fourteen of us.

One hundred and fourteen boys and girls would file every morning along pathways which led from the villages and the low-lying areas by the river, up our Alepino hill and into the school.

Our Alepino primary school with its four classes was built and opened in 1880. It had only two classrooms and another small room for the staff, of whom there were never more than two. The first and third years would be placed together in one classroom and taken by one teacher, whilst the second and fourth years would do their lessons in the second classroom with another teacher. By the way, when I was at school I was taught exclusively by women teachers.

From the outside the school was a small, single-storey, wood-clad building, painted with red lead. Two pines rose above the building, evidently they had been planted when the school was built, and there was also a mighty birch which drooped its branches and wept like a weeping willow. You could say that limes too rose over the school, considering it was built close by the church fence where the limes grew, so that only a narrow passage, just wide enough to get through on a horse or in a cart, separated the school from the church fence. Then, around the school, was the village green, an even sward on to which all one hundred and fourteen children poured during the 'break' to run, play, fight and tumble.

The village children found it hard to get used quickly to school discipline (sitting in one place for forty-five minutes), and I recall how Shurka Moskovkina got out

146

from behind her desk in the middle of a lesson and set off for the exit.

'Moskovkina! Where are you going? Go straight back to your place,' the mistress said sternly, raising her voice.

'I want a pasty,' admitted Shurka disarmingly.

They tried hard, of course, to teach us reading and writing. They taught us arithmetic, they taught us geography and we learnt all about the map (the Chukchi, Nenets, Lopari and Kamchadal peoples). The map had disproportionately large, bold black squares, rectangles and circles to indicate minerals, but alongside that, and I think against the will and inclination of the teachers, there was the business of processing the children's brains and souls. The District Education Department made them – ordered them – to do it, and so after lessons all four classes found themselves gathered together learning songs and singing them in chorus whilst sitting at their desks:

> The Five-Year Plan is on this chart,
> Let's look and see what we can learn,
> Where factories were far apart,
> Now they are seen at every turn.

Sometimes the songs had a little more bite to them:

> Soon this gang will fall before us
> And the victors we will be,
> Just red heroes will be glorious,
> Just red eagles, such as we.

And in lessons devoted to our native language, where we should have been learning to recite 'My Little Bluebells, Flowers of the Steppe', 'A Lone White Sail Is Showing', or at least something from 'Little Hump-backed Horse',[33] we were actually repeating mindlessly after the teacher: 'And in our fields are tractors, tractors. . . .' In other words, the collective-farm fields were being contrasted with a field belonging to a private individual in which a

147

ploughman would be working with a plough and horse. 'You search in vain, Nikita's grain, deep in the ground, cannot be found.' Here the meaning is clear enough. When they were forcibly taking away the peasants' grain without paying for it, that is to say, to put it simply, when they were robbing them of it, the villain Nikita hid his grain so that his family would not starve to death afterwards, the way more than seven million people died of hunger in 1933 in the Ukraine and the Volga Region.

Some Katya Barsukova would recite in her perky little voice:

> A song about metal is sounding,
> Throughout the whole land hear it swell,
> More steel, more steel they're demanding,
> More copper and iron as well.

And your humble servant, who began with Lermontov and Pushkin under the guidance of Katyusha, as perhaps will be remembered, recited the following on the 21st January, a day, as is well known, of mourning,[34] at a school Open Evening held in honour of that day (evidently even then I knew how to recite – that is, to declaim verse):

> Shake, tyrants of the world, before us,
> For Lenin lives on even now,
> You never will be victors o'er us,
> In us does Lenin's spirit glow.

In school then they concentrated on stupefying and cluttering up our brains, but what happened at home? What was my mother doing, my religious mother who loved and knew Nekrasov, Koltsov and Surikov by heart? What was my sister, who introduced me to A.K. Tolstoy, Pushkin and Lermontov, doing? Well, never mind about my sister. By that time she was living in Moscow and attending courses run by the RRC (Russian Red Cross) – in other words to put it simply, she was studying to be a nurse.

But my mother. . . . My parents, who clearly understood that I would have to live my whole life surrounded by Soviet power, obviously allowed themselves to be guided by an instinct for self-preservation and stayed well away from my, so to speak, social upbringing, preferring to entrust me to the Soviet school. What is more, even at home they gave every support to the sort of education I was getting at school. At any rate, when, moved by a feeling which was almost religious in its strength and vividness, I began to put together a 'Lenin Corner' at home and fixed a mass of photographs of Lenin to the wall, beginning with the curly-haired boy and ending with the coffin and Mausoleum, no one in the family stopped me and no one saw or heard the rubbing of hands, the gloating and sniggering that was going on at the time behind my left shoulder, nor the sadness, if not weeping, at my right.

NOTES

TRANSLATOR'S NOTES EXCEPT AS INDICATED

1 The Day of the Holy Trinity is not the equivalent of Trinity Sunday but the seventh Sunday after Easter: Whit Sunday or Pentecost.

2 In the Russian 'about a hundred buckets'. The tub was indeed large. The bucket was a unit of capacity equal to approximately twenty-one pints.

3 A style of decoration developed in the nineteenth century in the village of Zhostovo, Moscow Region. Its most characteristic feature is the use of floral designs on a black background.

4 The reference is to a ring owned by the author on which Tsar Nicholas II is depicted.

5 Such a process should not be confused, of course, with the kind of activity associated with usury, banking and parasitism, which you really cannot suspect tens of millions of well-established, prosperous Russian peasant farmers of engaging in. (Author's note).

6 The pood was a measure of weight used before the Revolution. It contained forty Russian pounds and was equal to 16.38 kilograms.

7 In standard Russian unstressed 'o' is pronounced as 'a' (cf. later in the narrative Lámanov/Lámonov, pronounced identically, hence the possible variation in spelling). In the area around Vladimir native to Soloukhin, however, the pronunciation of 'o' as 'o' is retained, and this can even – as is seen here – have an effect upon a genuine 'a'. The initial A of Andrey is 'corrected' to O, the spelling here, in all probability reflecting the actual pronunciation.

8 Stesha: familiar and affectionate form of Stepanida.

9 Strictly speaking, my Karavaevo grandfather's surname was Elagin. However, in Pokrov, the quiet provincial town that acted as a magnet for Karavaevo, there was a cabman called Cheburov who was famous for the dashing way he drove; and my grandfather, Ivan Mikhaylovich Elagin, was also a fast, efficient worker. One or two people said to him: 'Well, friend, you certainly can work! You're a real Cheburov!' This nickname stuck and afterwards, surprising as it may

seem, became Grandfather's surname and, therefore, my mother's maiden name. (Author's note).

10 The fact that the small villages are all disappearing from the face of the earth and being ploughed under, whereas the bigger ones still somehow manage to survive, does not contradict this rule. (Author's note).

11 The form Olepino is used in place of Alepino as an indication of local pronunciation (see note 7 above).

12 Cosmas and Damian: physicians and wonderworkers from Asia Minor. Martyred at the end of the third century, they are the patron saints of physicians. Their feast-day is celebrated by the Orthodox Church on 14th November.

13 Lámonov: see note 7 above.

14 Again, in order to get an idea of the proportions involved, let's just think: the drawing-room with the decorated walls could not have been more than thirty square metres – most likely even less. (Author's note).

15 pood: see note 6 above.

16 'Quarters' was the name given to the three-litre bottles that were in wide use. (Author's note).

17 Mikhail Mikhaylovich Prishvin (1873–1954), writer, naturalist and ethnographer. In his work he subtly linked vivid descriptions of life and nature with a message concerning the ethics of love and creativity.

18 The long-awaited 'Maria' appears in the poem 'A Cloud in Trousers' (1915) by Vladimir Vladimirovich Mayakovsky (1893–1930).

19 Aleksey Konstantinovich Tolstoy (1817–75), lyric poet, historical novelist and dramatist. In his work he frequently attacked bureaucracy and tyranny.

20 Lámanovs: see note 7 above.

21 Not Joseph's dream but a dream of Pharaoh's which Joseph interpreted (Genesis 41: 14–36).

22 Poltava is in the Ukraine, some seven hundred kilometres south-west of Moscow.

23 The *desyatsky* was the lowest-ranking administrative official in Tsarist Russia. The name is derived from the word for 'ten', as in theory every ten households would provide one *desyatsky*. The *desyatskies* performed general police duties.

24 *Znamia* = The Banner.

25 The 9th Congress of the Russian Communist Party

(Bolsheviks) took place in March–April 1920 not 1921.

26 SSR: Soviet Socialist Republic.

27 'Dizzy with Success': an article published by Stalin in March 1930 in which he blamed local officials for the waste of livestock and equipment during collectivization as well as for the decline in popular support for the government.

28 Mikhail Ivanovich Kalinin (1875–1946), Soviet statesman, was head of state in the years 1919–46.

29 The author's intention is that the present volume should form the first part of a two-part autobiography.

30 Alexander Aleksandrovich Blok (1880–1921), Russia's most famous Symbolist poet, lived during his formative years at Shakhmatovo, an estate near Moscow owned by his maternal grandfather, A.N. Beketov, botanist and Rector of St Petersburg University.

31 Peter the Great gave instructions that Russian church bells be melted down to make cannons at the beginning of the Great Northern War (1700–21), after the Russians had been defeated by the Swedes at the Battle of Narva (1700).

32 Alexander Alekseevich Zharov (1904–84) and Alexander Ilyich Bezymensky (1898–1973) were both poets who wrote politically inspired verse. Bezymensky, at one time an official of the Writers' Union, wrote on the theme of collectivization and was personally championed by Stalin.

33 'Little Hump-backed Horse': title of a fairy-tale in verse written in 1834 by the poet, playwright and short-story writer, Petr Petrovich Ershov (1815–69).

34 Vladimir Lenin died on 21st January 1924.